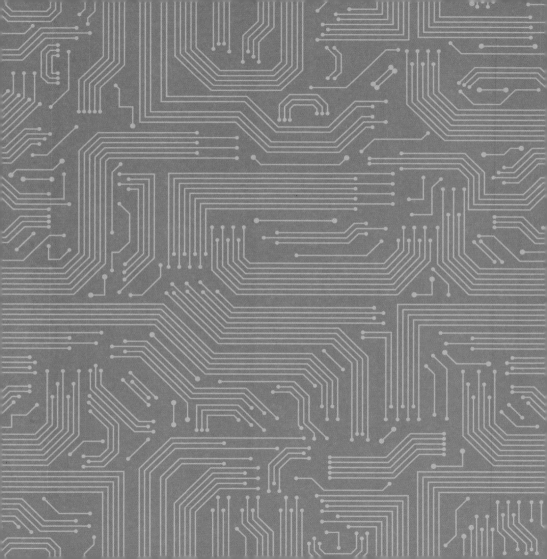

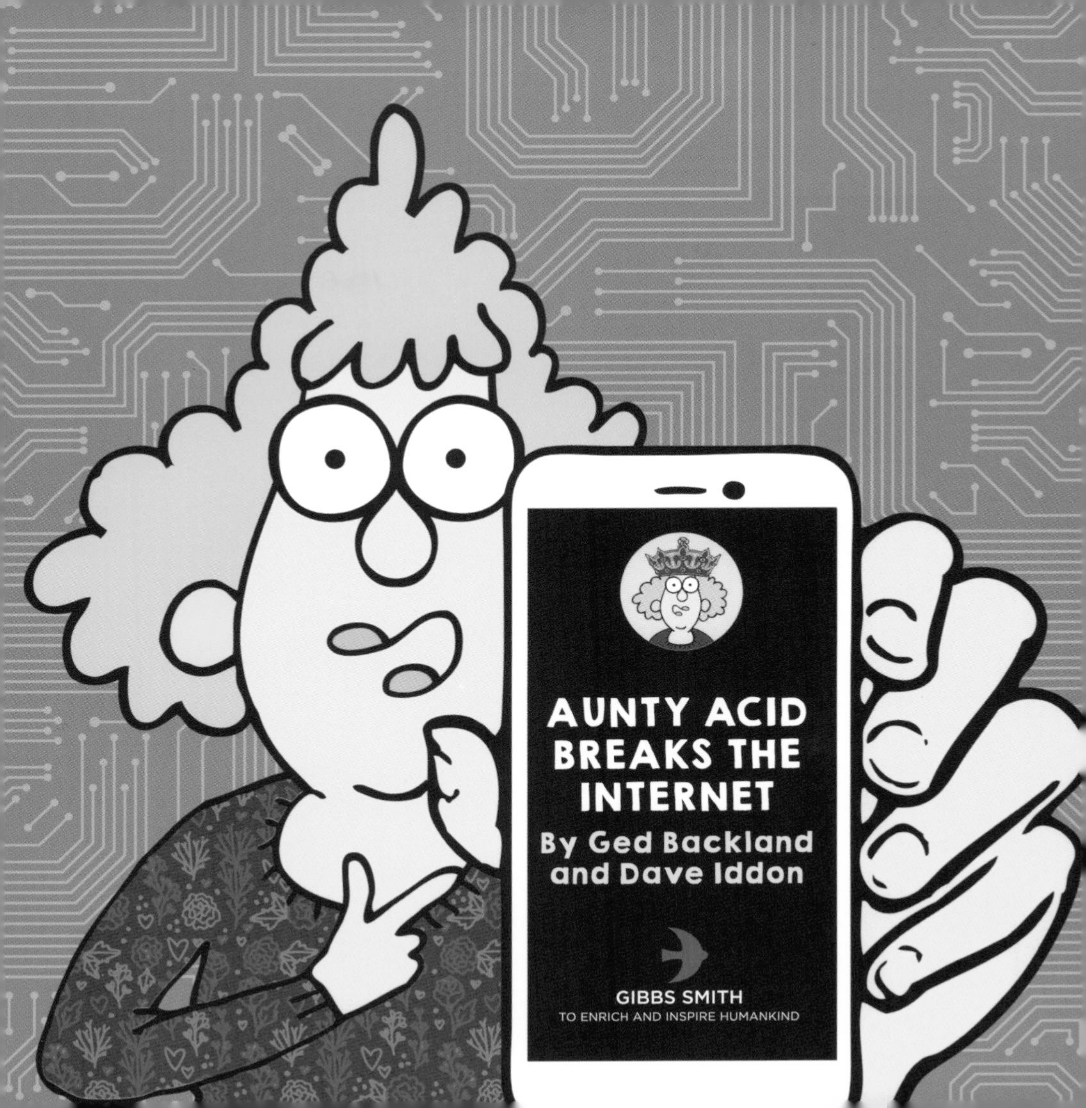

AUNTY ACID BREAKS THE INTERNET
By Ged Backland and Dave Iddon
GIBBS SMITH
TO ENRICH AND INSPIRE HUMANKIND

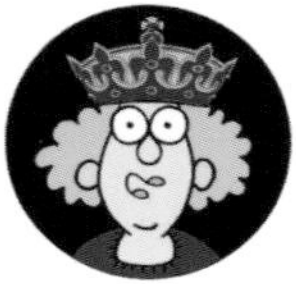

Dear loyal internet subjects,

The Queen of social media here (psst—that's me, Aunty Acid)

Many apologies if you're having trouble connecting to the interweb today, for I seem to have broken it. No, not with my big ole butt like one of the Kardashian sisters, I pressed the wrong freakin' button and now it won't come back on.

Please HELP! If it doesn't start working soon I'll have to go and speak to all those people who live in my house. I think they're called "my family" and they seem, well, kinda annoying actually!

While we're waiting to get back online, why don't we have a li'l conversation about all things social? Did you know they now have fridges that connect to Facebook? They're called smart fridges, but it's yet to slap me every time I go and get another bottle of wine, so it can't be that freakin' clever can it?

Either way, we now we have smart fridges, smart TVs, and smart phones... I wish they'd just get around to making smart people!

Seriously, it seems like these days you can choose to be whoever you want to be online, but most people are choosing to be stupid.

So please join me for the following pages on all things internet, from social media's biggest questions to the perils of internet dating and not forgetting the best tips on hiding all your internet shopping from your husband.

Now go forth and filter!

Your Social Media Queen,

Aunty A x

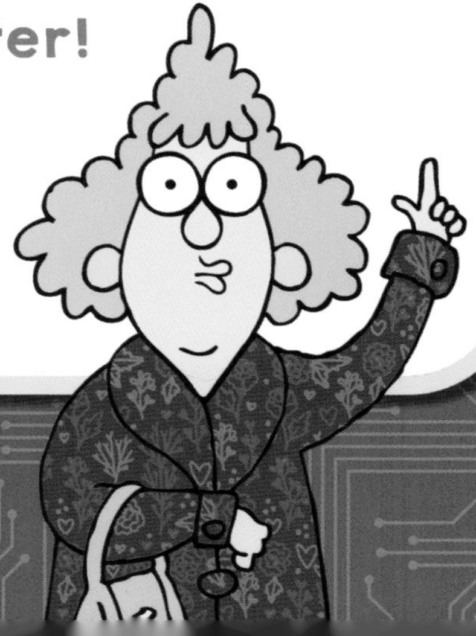

SOCIAL MEDIA

has become a contest of who can pull their bathing costume up their ass the farthest.

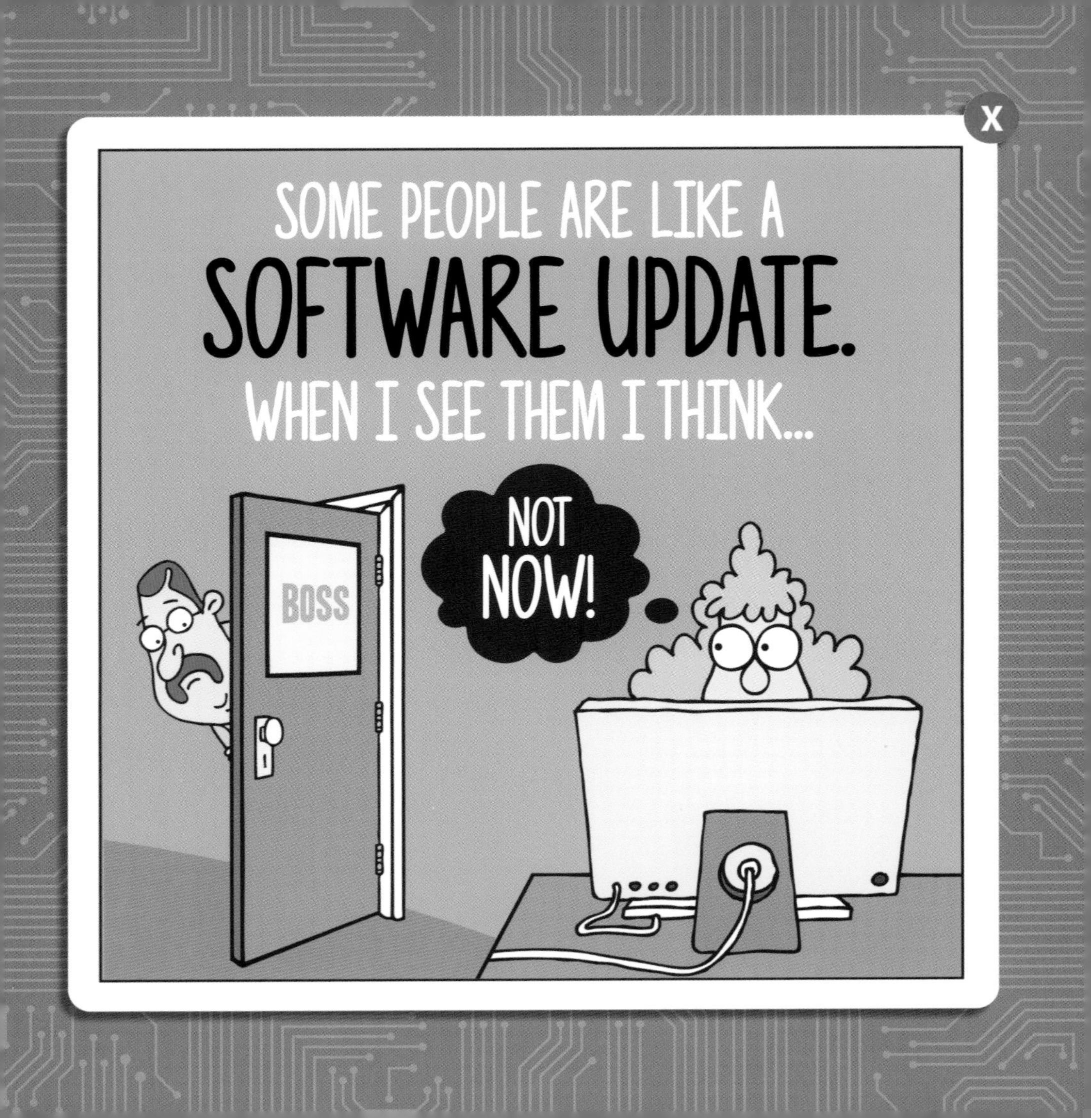
SOME PEOPLE ARE LIKE A
SOFTWARE UPDATE.
WHEN I SEE THEM I THINK...
X
BOSS
NOT NOW!

I wish Facebook would notify me when someone unfriends me. You know, so I could freakin' LIKE IT.

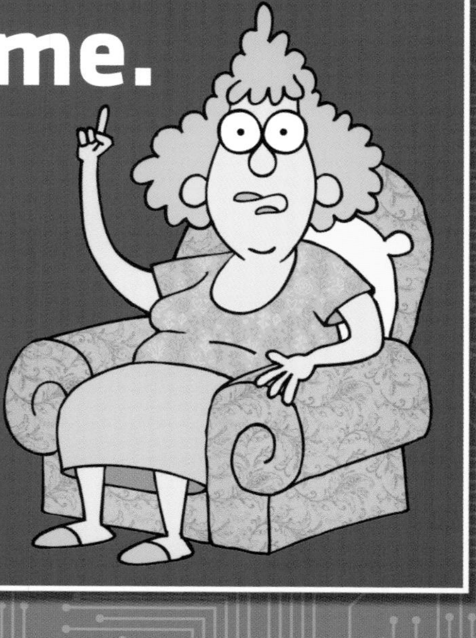

This is my
SELFIE STICK.

If I see someone taking a selfie,

I HIT THEM WITH IT.

HEY YOU!

STOP POSTING YOUR
PROBLEMS ON
FACEBOOK AND
DRINK ALCOHOL
LIKE THE REST OF US.

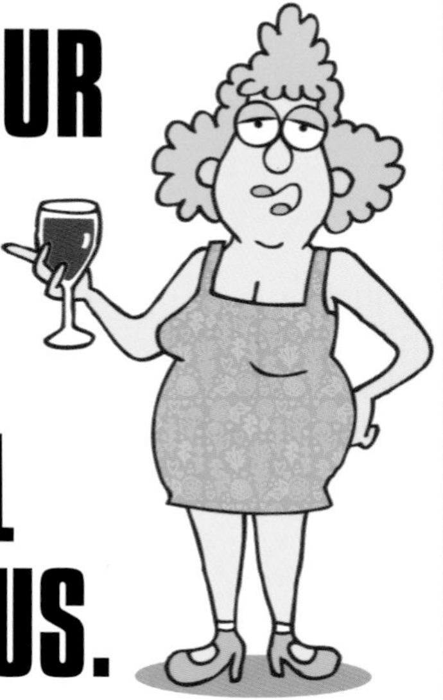

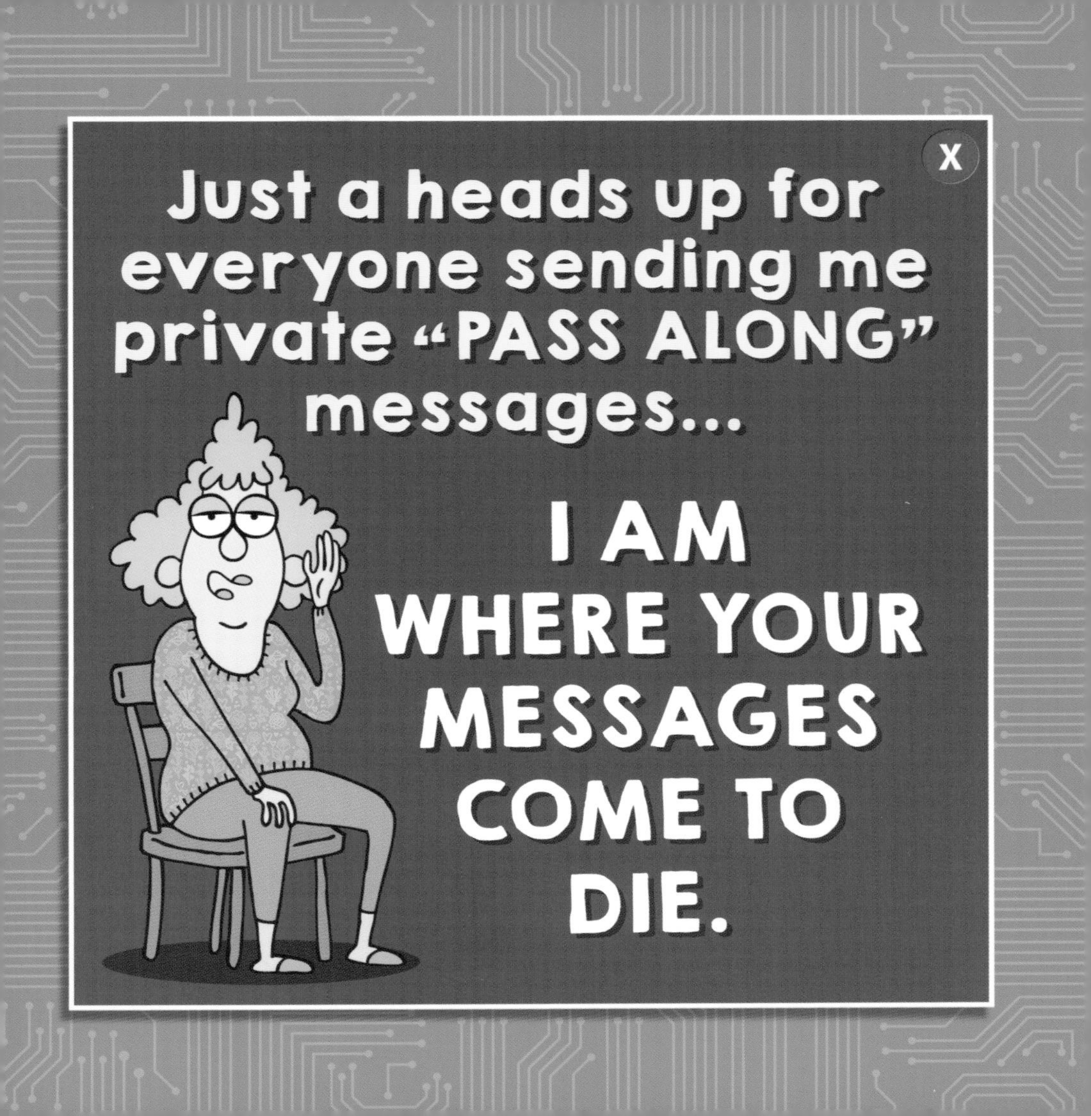
X
Just a heads up for everyone sending me private "PASS ALONG" messages...
I AM WHERE YOUR MESSAGES COME TO DIE.

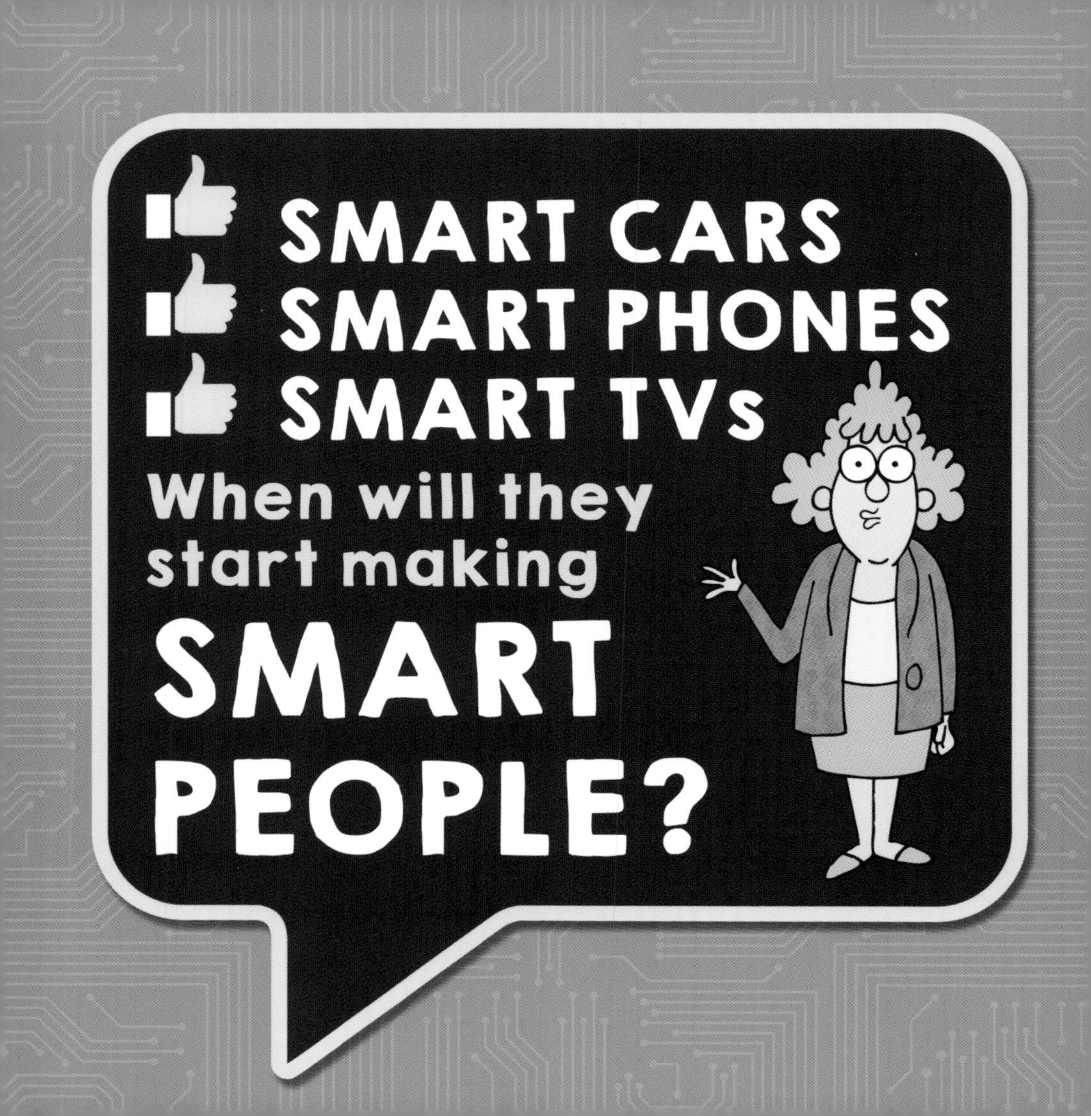
SMART CARS
SMART PHONES
SMART TVs
When will they start making
SMART PEOPLE?

HOW MANY APPLES DOES IT TAKE TO KEEP EVERYONE AWAY?

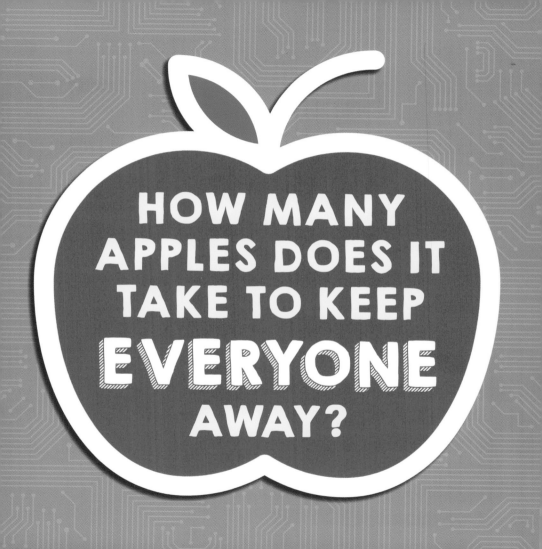

AT MY AGE, I CAN SEND A TEXT AT 10:34 AND BE ASLEEP AT 10:34:19

DON'T BOTHER PAYING A **THERAPIST.**

I'LL TELL YOU WHAT'S WRONG WITH YOU FOR FREE.

ATTENTION!

LIFE HAS NO REMOTE

SO GET UP AND DO IT YOURSELF

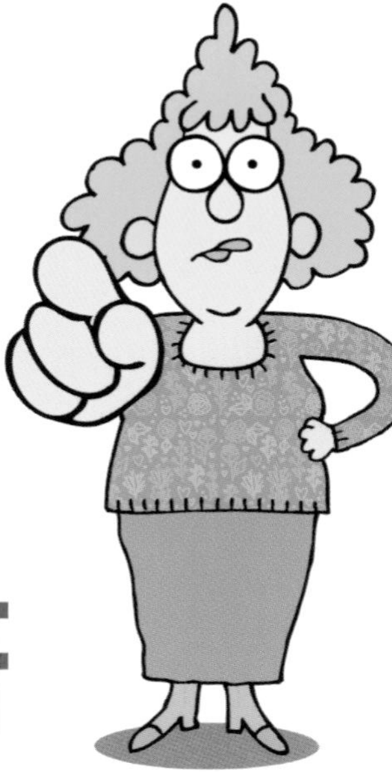

Please note that I am

SELF-EMPLOYED.

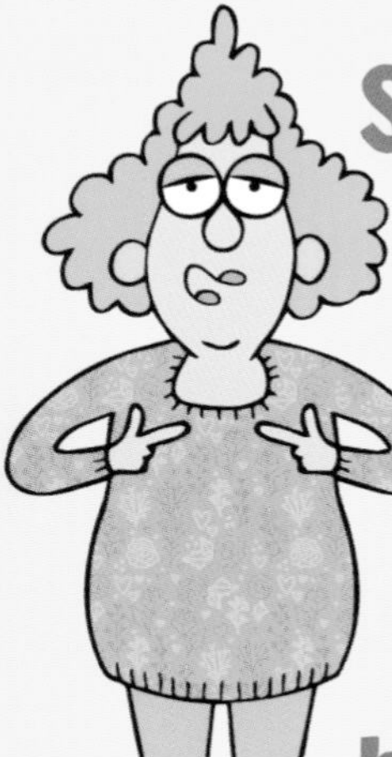

So if you see me talking to myself

PLEASE DO NOT DISTURB ME

because I'm having a staff meeting.

AUNTY'S

A-Z

of
SOCIAL MEDIA

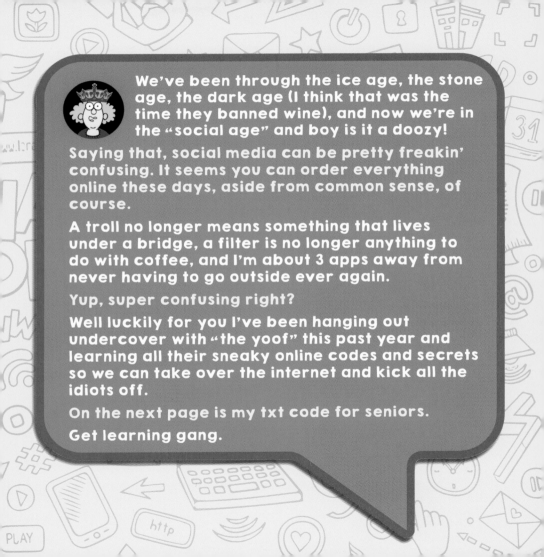

We've been through the ice age, the stone age, the dark age (I think that was the time they banned wine), and now we're in the "social age" and boy is it a doozy!

Saying that, social media can be pretty freakin' confusing. It seems you can order everything online these days, aside from common sense, of course.

A troll no longer means something that lives under a bridge, a filter is no longer anything to do with coffee, and I'm about 3 apps away from never having to go outside ever again.

Yup, super confusing right?

Well luckily for you I've been hanging out undercover with "the yoof" this past year and learning all their sneaky online codes and secrets so we can take over the internet and kick all the idiots off.

On the next page is my txt code for seniors.

Get learning gang.

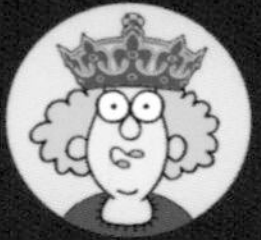

AUNTY ACID'S TEXT CODE FOR SENIORS:

LOL - Little old lady
GOM - Grumpy old man
GGA - Got gas again
FWIW - Forgot where I was
PIMP - Pooped in my pants
BYOT - Bring your own teeth
TTYL - Talk to you louder
CUATSC - See you at the senior center
SGGP - Sorry gotta go poop
ROFLACGU - Rolling on floor laughing and can't get up

For those who don't want ALEXA listening in on your conversations,

they're making a male version.

It doesn't listen to anything.

Apparently the CIA can hack into my TV and listen to every word I say...

but McDonald's can't hear me say, "NO PICKLES" through their drive-thru speaker.

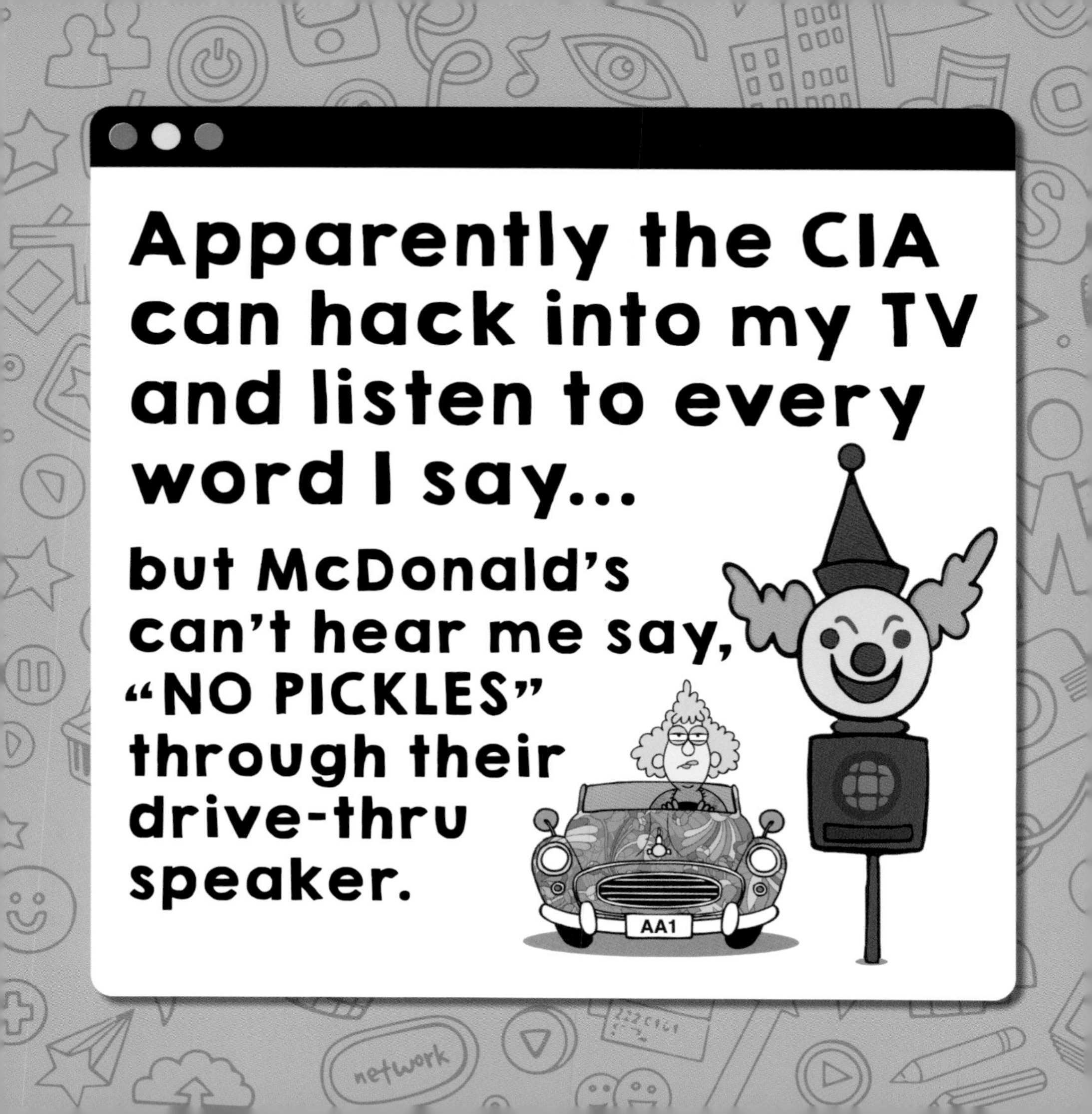
AA1

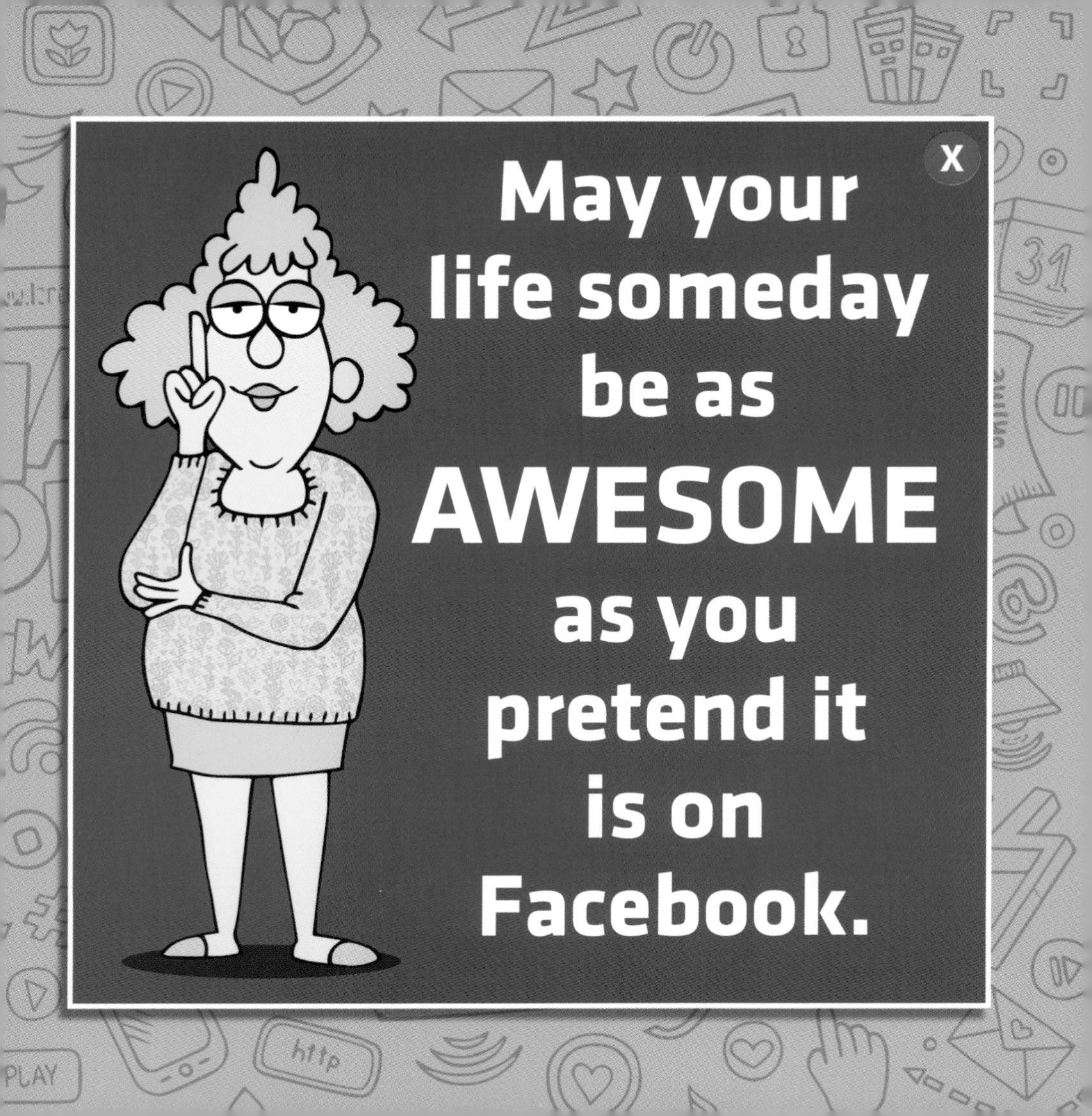
May your life someday be as AWESOME as you pretend it is on Facebook.

I haven't got a Twitter account, so I just carry around a **MEGAPHONE** to announce what I'm doing every 30 minutes.

I've got 3 followers so far, but I think 2 of them are cops.

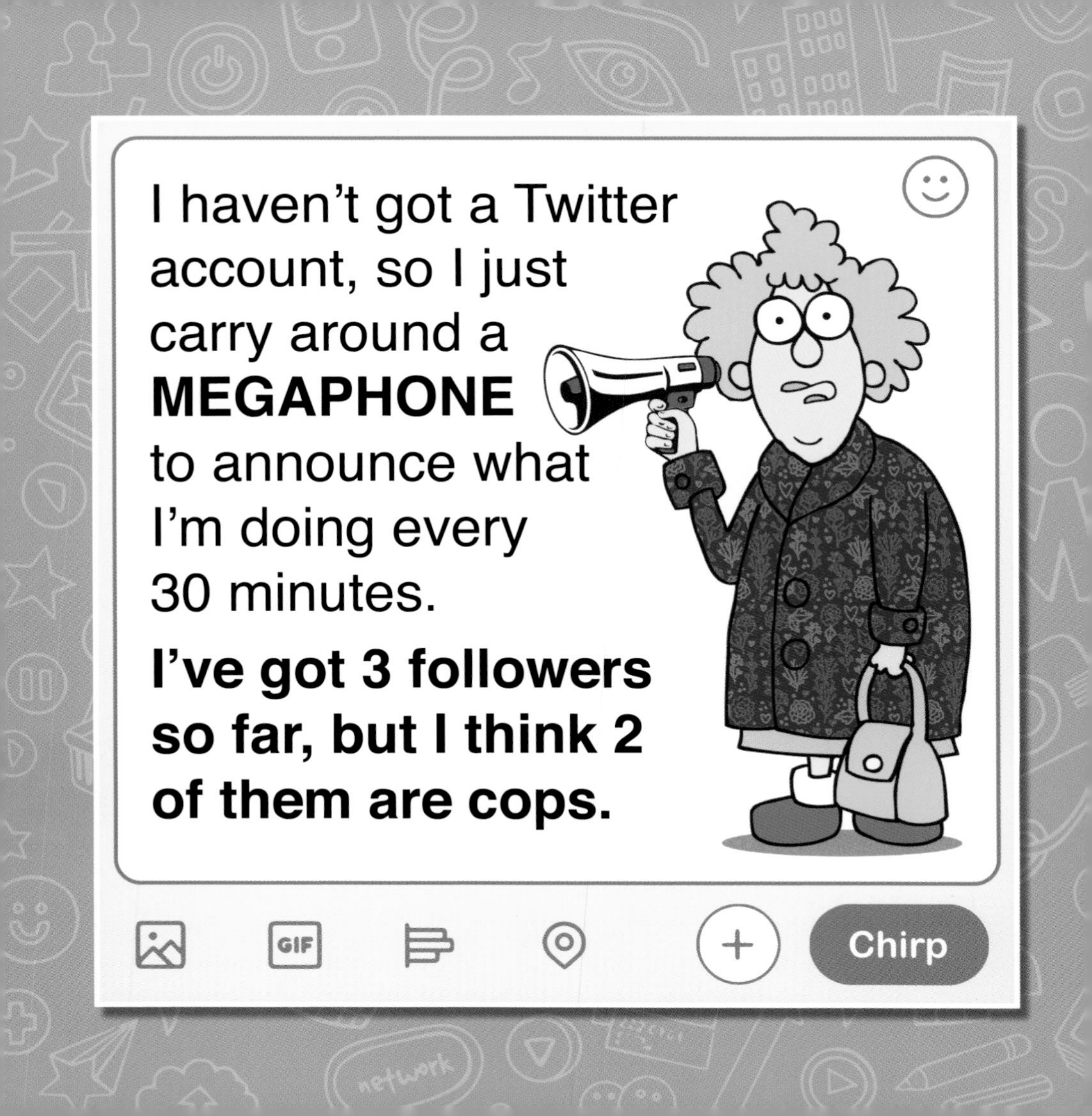

GIF

Chirp

⚠️ **FYI**

Your dirty laundry belongs in the

WASHING MACHINE, not on FACEBOOK

Logging onto Facebook has become the equivalent of opening the fridge door and staring inside even though you're not hungry.

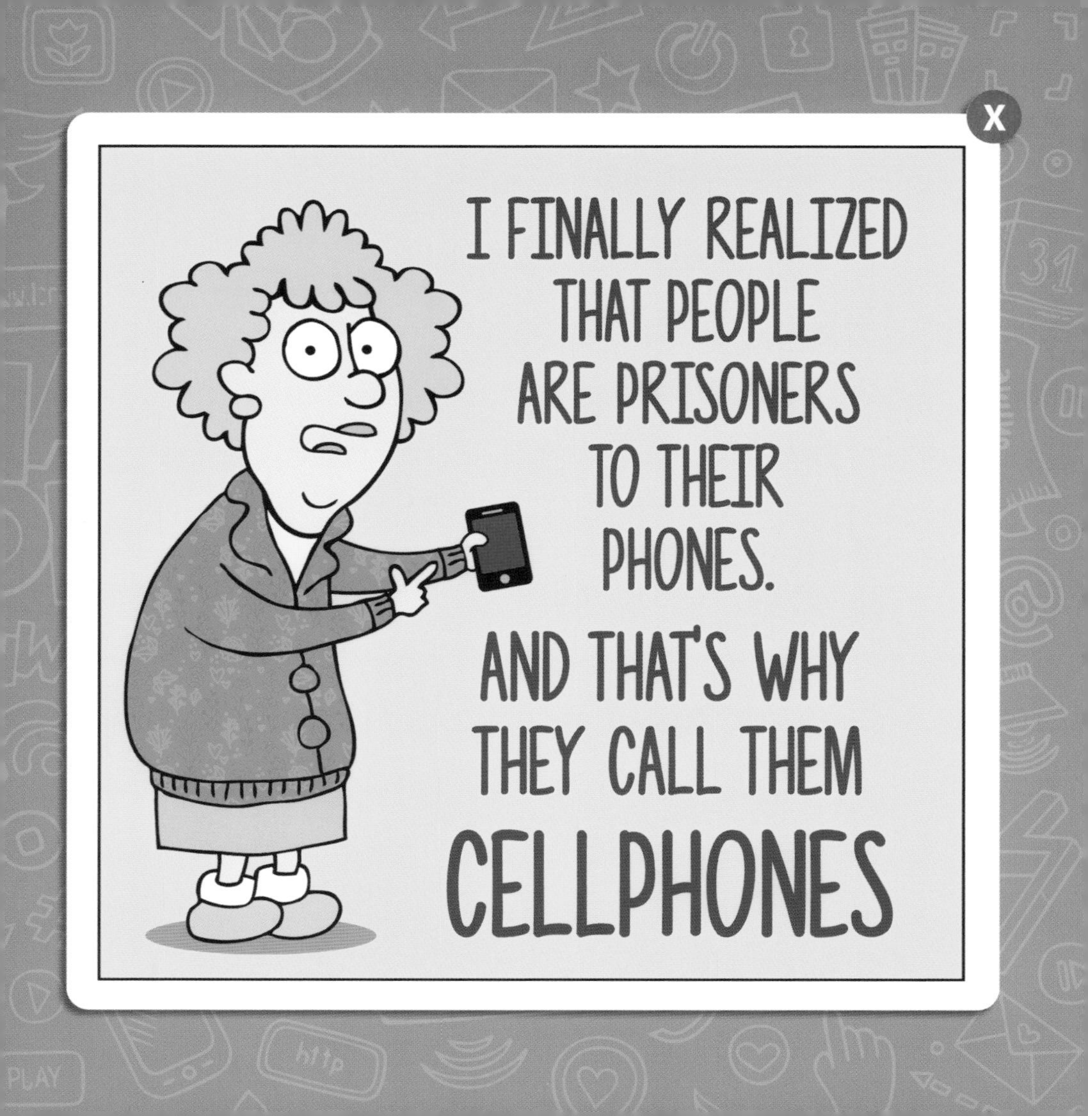
X
I FINALLY REALIZED THAT PEOPLE ARE PRISONERS TO THEIR PHONES.
AND THAT'S WHY THEY CALL THEM CELLPHONES
PLAY
http

The adult version of “HEADS, SHOULDERS, KNEES AND TOES” is “WALLET, GLASSES, KEYS AND PHONE.”

I LOVE
Google
IT'S LIKE
THE BRAIN I
DON'T HAVE

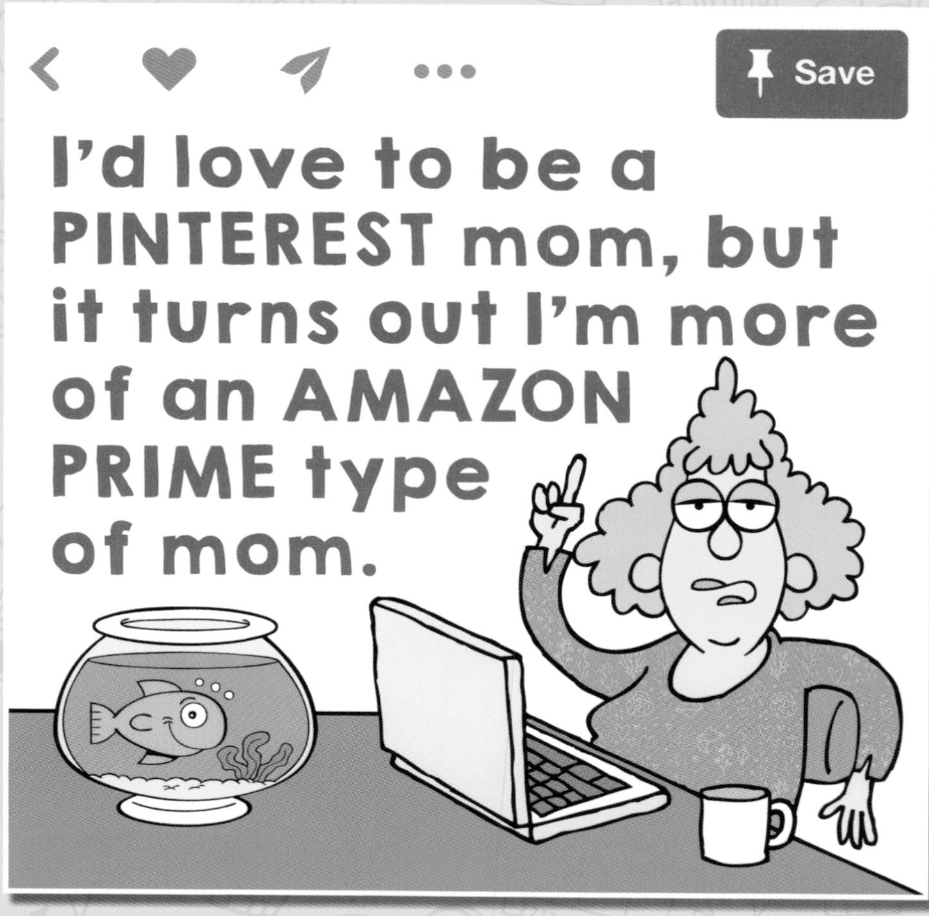
Save
I'd love to be a PINTEREST mom, but it turns out I'm more of an AMAZON PRIME type of mom.

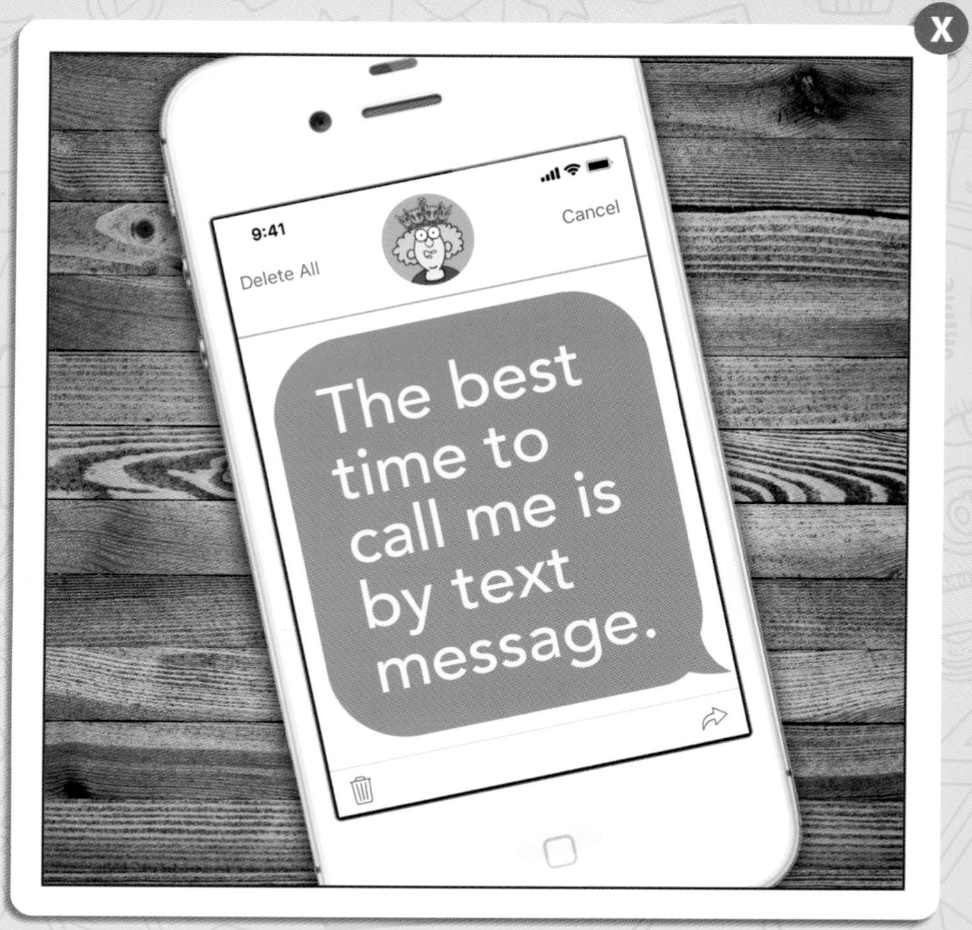
9:41
Cancel
Delete All
The best time to call me is by text message.

Nothing starts my day off quite like when I give inspirational messages to my friends...

MAY YOUR DAY GO FAST, YOUR SOCKS MATCH, AND YOUR UNDERWEAR NOT RIDE UP YOUR BUTT.

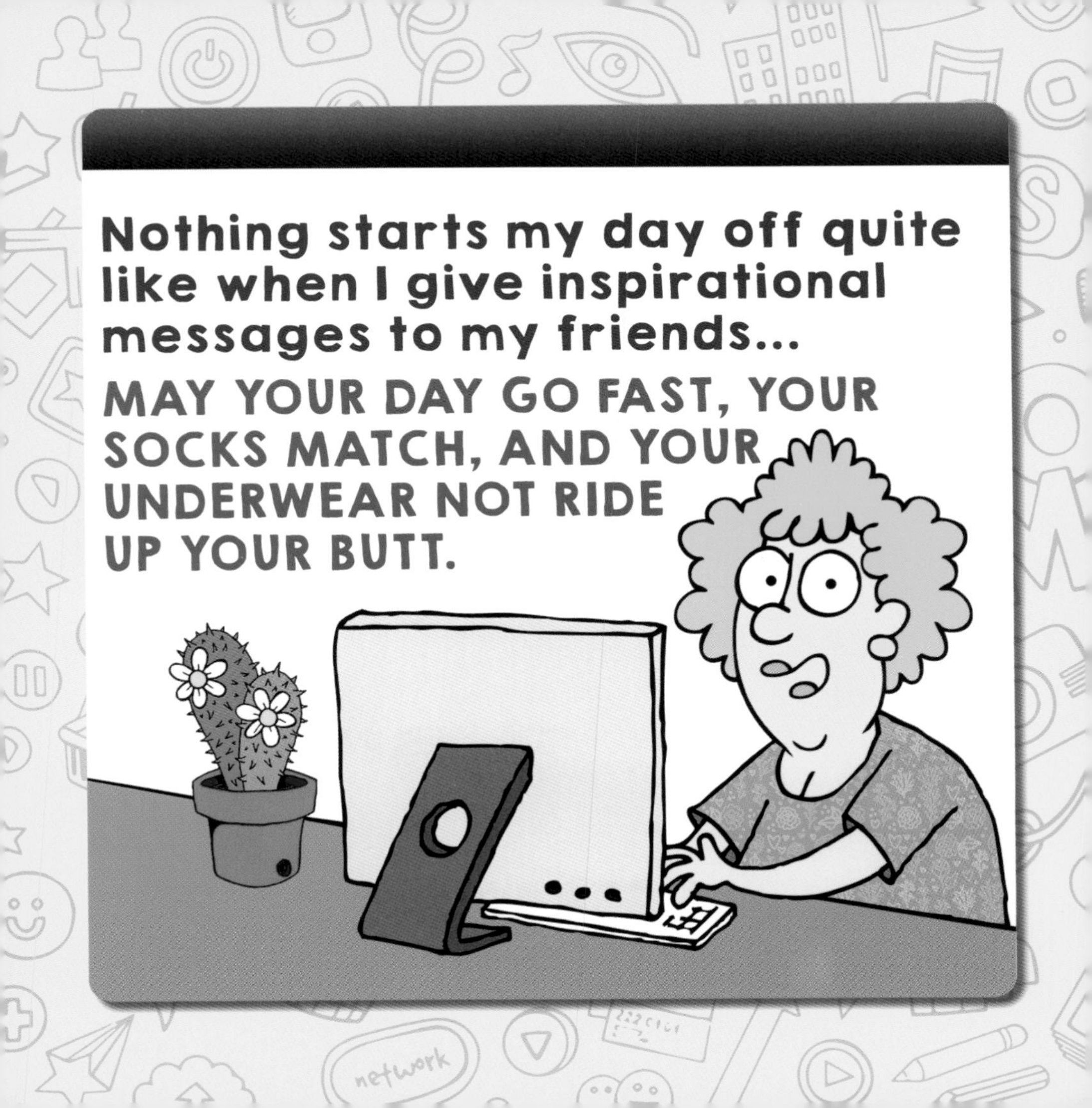

"AS PER MY LAST EMAIL"

is office speak for

"CAN'T YOU READ, DUMB-ASS?!"

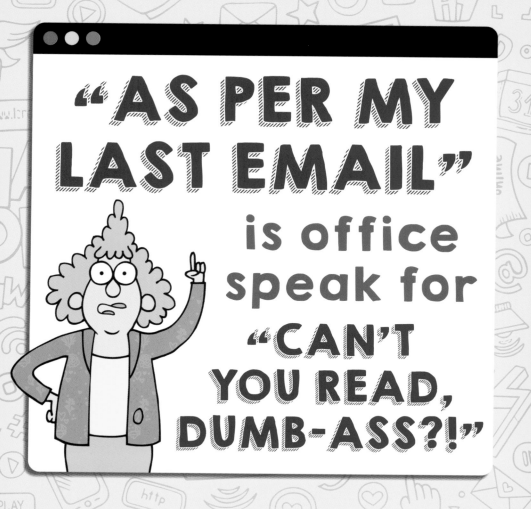

SELFIES
ARE A LOT
SADDER
WHEN YOU
THINK OF
THEM AS
ALONE-IES

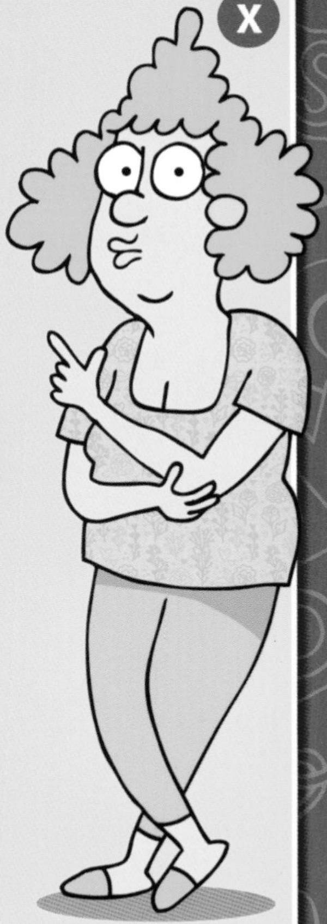

HOW TO BE A GREAT FRIEND:

👍 Show up with wine.

👍 Make me laugh.

👍 Keep my secrets.

👍 Delete all the embarrassing stuff on my phone if I unexpectedly die.

We may call it
"SOCIAL" MEDIA
but I know that
I spend half
my time
using it
alone or on
the freakin'
toilet.

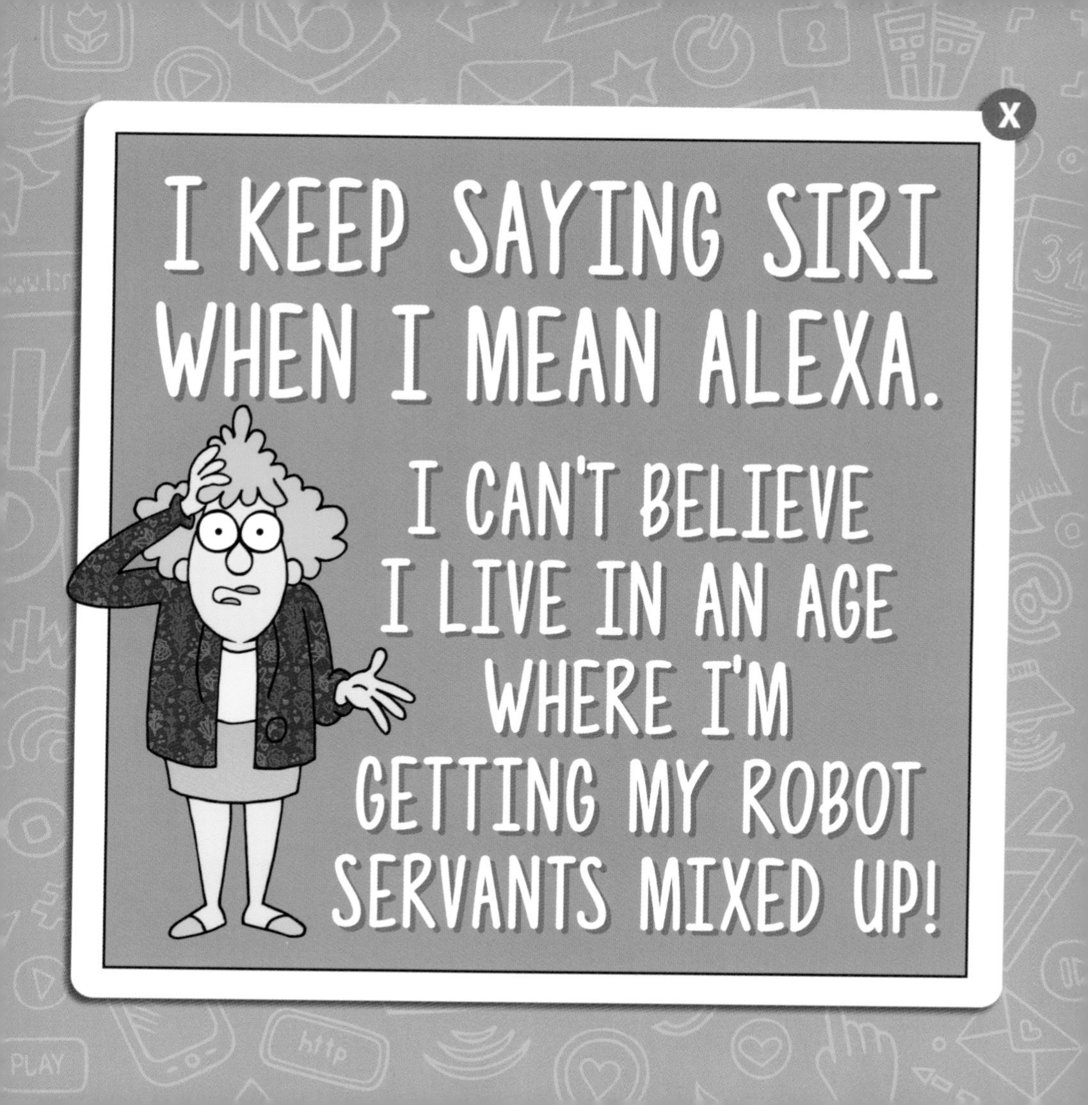
I KEEP SAYING SIRI WHEN I MEAN ALEXA.
I CAN'T BELIEVE I LIVE IN AN AGE WHERE I'M GETTING MY ROBOT SERVANTS MIXED UP!
X
PLAY
http

⚠️ FYI

If you can't say it to my face, then your

FACEBOOK BALLS

ain't gonna make a difference.

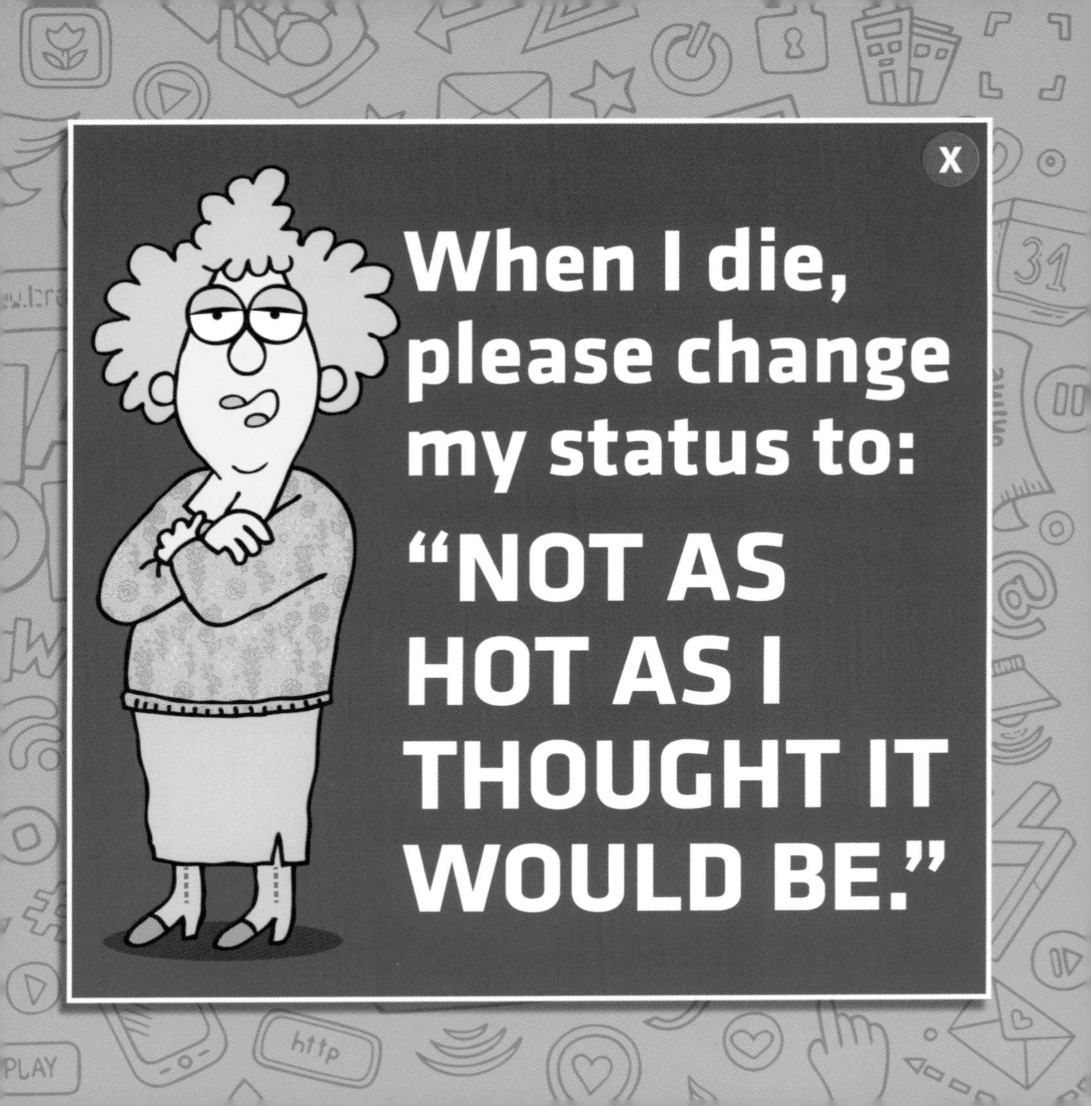

When I die, please change my status to:

“NOT AS HOT AS I THOUGHT IT WOULD BE.”

ONLINE DATING

Ahhh, online dating...

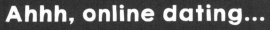

I don't know about you, but being an old romantic, I liked it better when you had to be in the same room as someone to see their genitals...

"Send nudes." How about send foods instead?

Being married for over 1000 years, I missed out on all that dating app fun, but sometimes I help my best friend Aunty Dee "find matches" and let me tell you, it ain't pretty out there in the big wide web.

They say there's plenty more fish in the sea... Well the online dating sea is filled with radioactive waste and weird fish.

There's all kinds of online dating lingo out there too—catfishing, ghosting, bae—I can't keep up. All I know is if I was single I'd prefer to meet people the old-fashioned way...

THROUGH POOR JUDGEMENT AND TOO MUCH BOOZE.

WHEN YOU'RE SINGLE AND PEOPLE TELL YOU THERE'S PLENTY OF FISH IN THE SEA BUT YOUR INBOX LOOKS LIKE:

MailTips could not be retrieved.

Subject: Possible Match

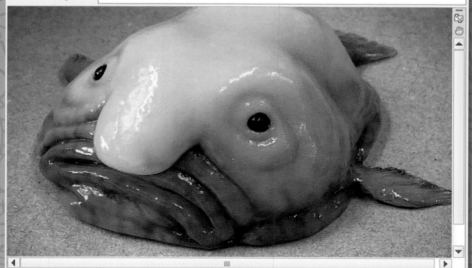

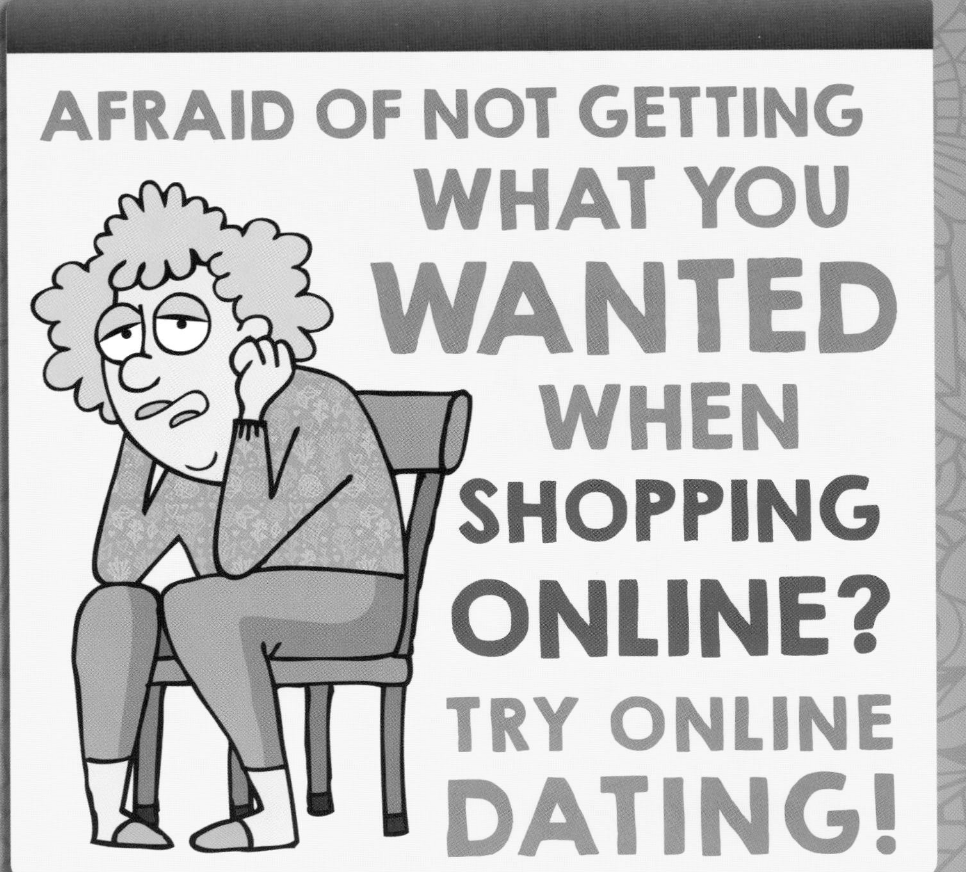
AFRAID OF NOT GETTING
WHAT YOU
WANTED
WHEN
SHOPPING
ONLINE?
TRY ONLINE
DATING!

EVER WONDERED HOW LONG FOREVER IS?

Well, looking at some people's FACEBOOK RELATIONSHIPS, it appears to be around 2 to 4 weeks.

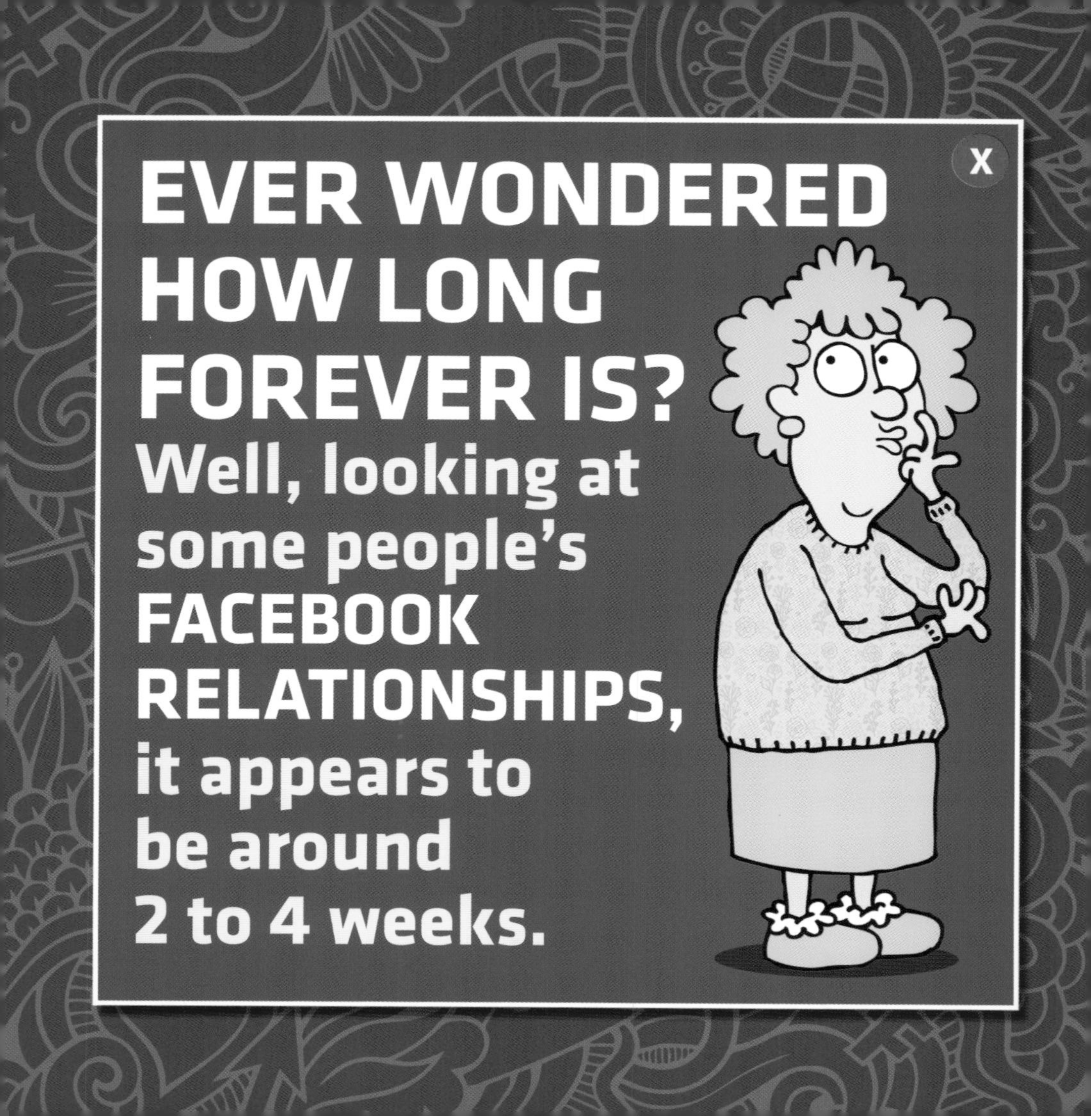

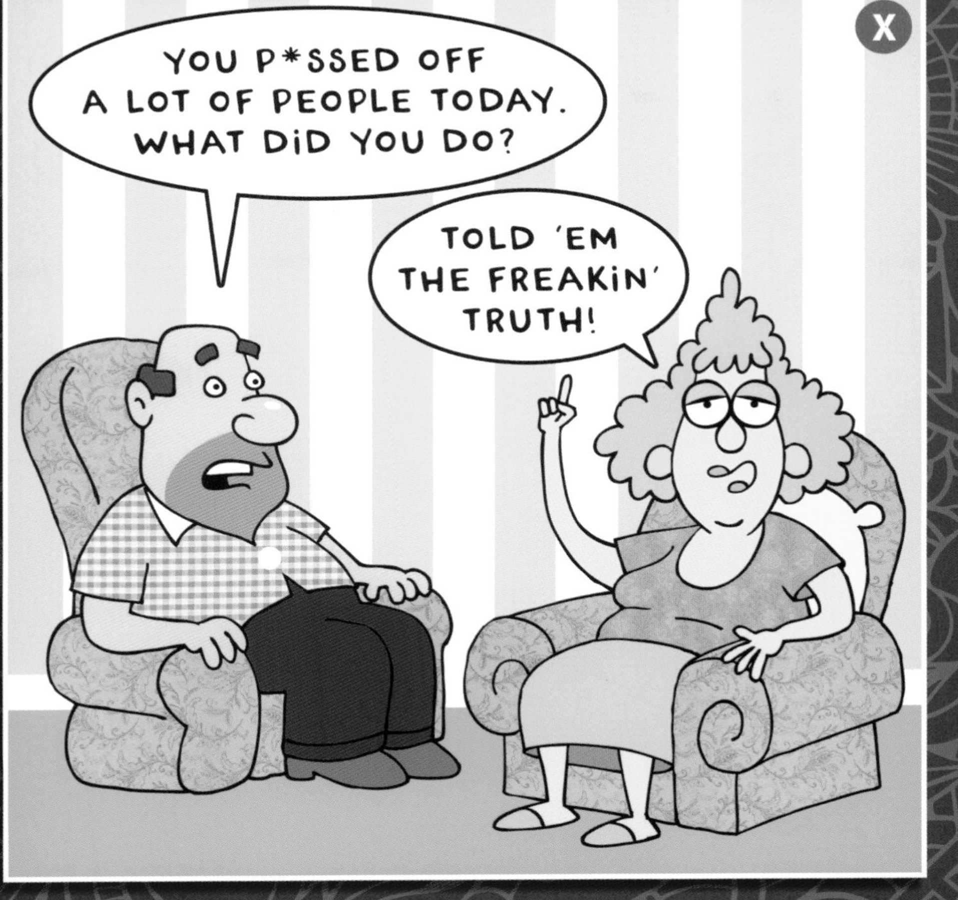
X
YOU P*SSED OFF A LOT OF PEOPLE TODAY. WHAT DID YOU DO?
TOLD 'EM THE FREAKIN' TRUTH!

STOP COMPLAINING ABOUT YOUR LIFE.

THERE ARE PEOPLE OUT THERE DATING YOUR EX!

Sometimes you might feel all alone and like no one's there for you.

You know who will always be there for you?

LAUNDRY.

Laundry will always be there for you.

I'M NOT ANTISOCIAL I'M JUST NOT USER FRIENDLY

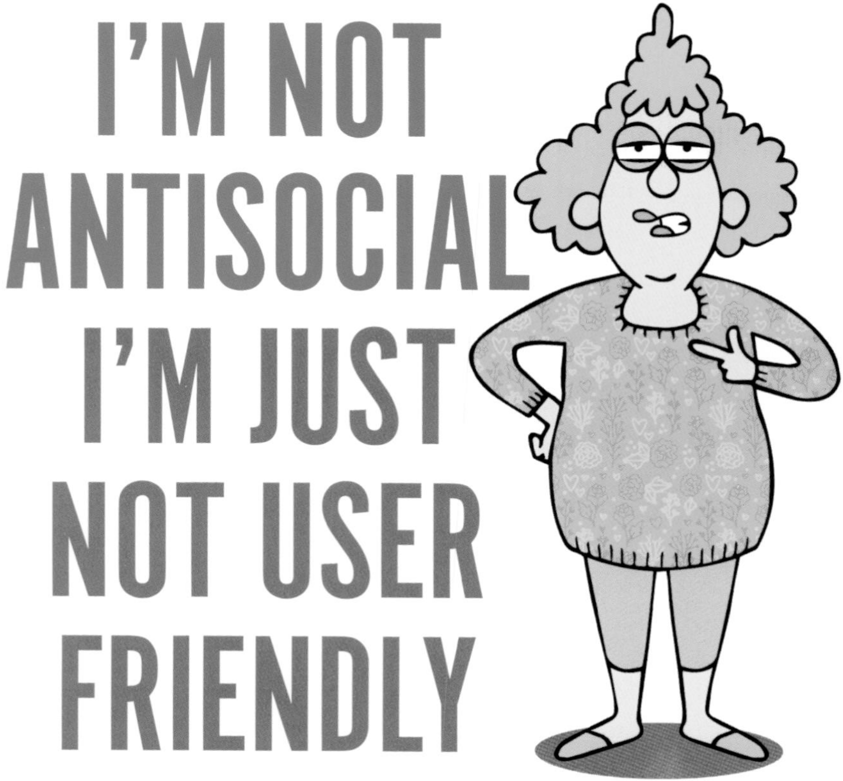

"Don't you wish someone would invent an idiot repellent?"

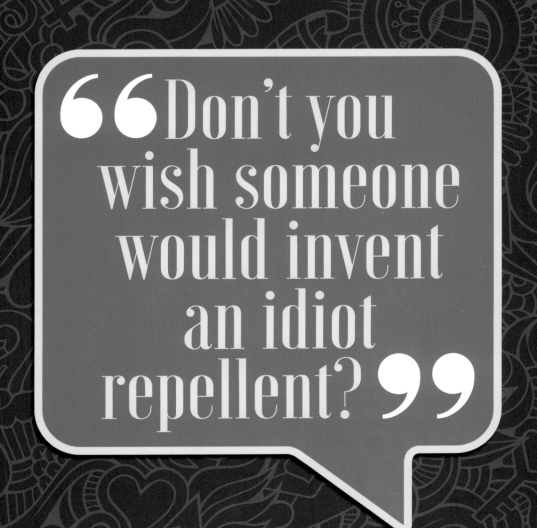

SURE, FACEBOOK STALKING IS ALL FUN AND GAMES

until you accidentally press the

LIKE BUTTON.

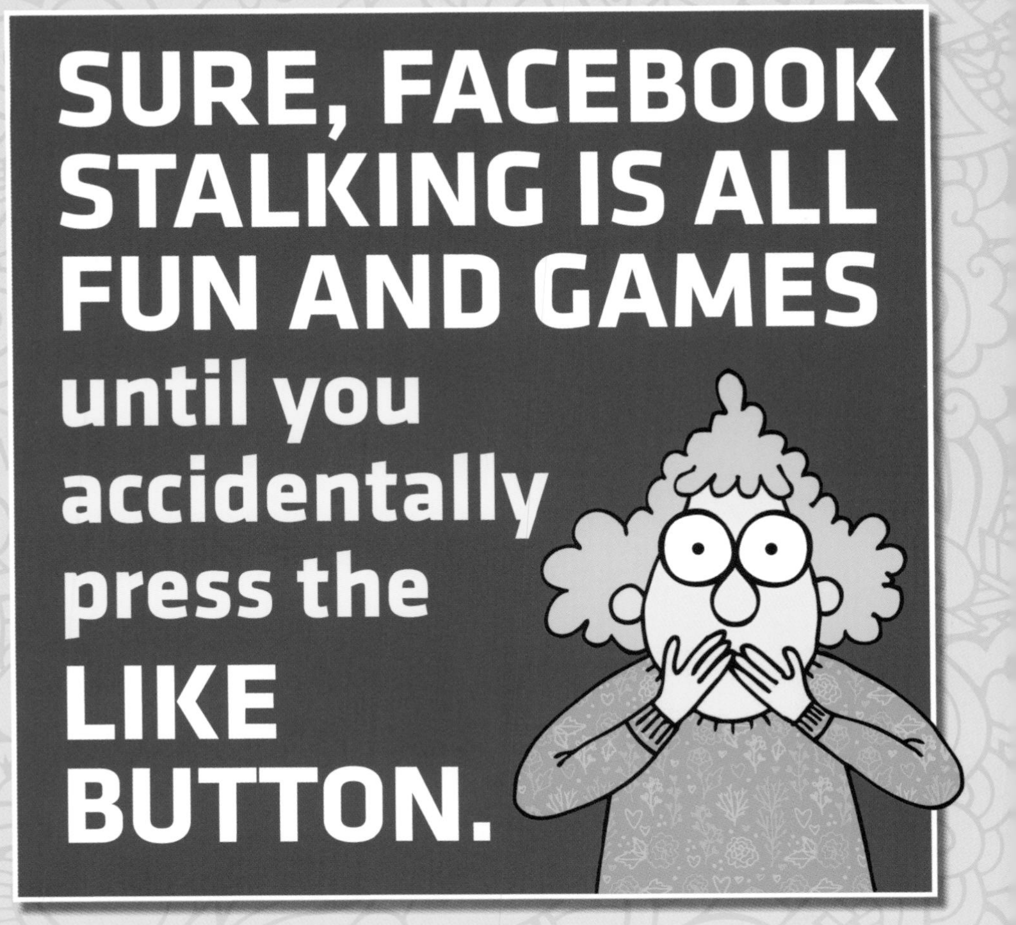

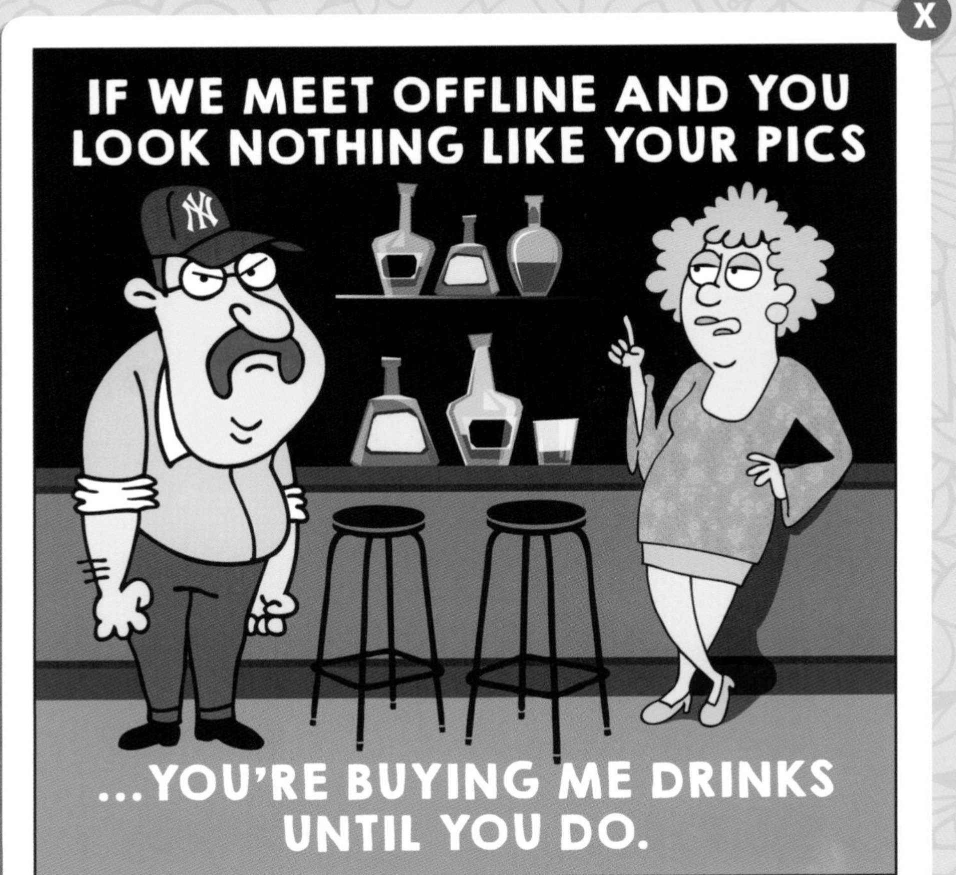
IF WE MEET OFFLINE AND YOU LOOK NOTHING LIKE YOUR PICS
NY
...YOU'RE BUYING ME DRINKS UNTIL YOU DO.
X

Not every FRIEND REQUEST is a friend request. Some are SURVEILLANCE CAMERAS.

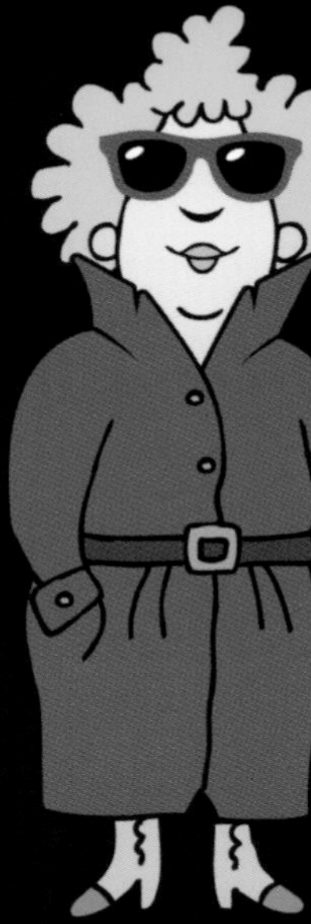

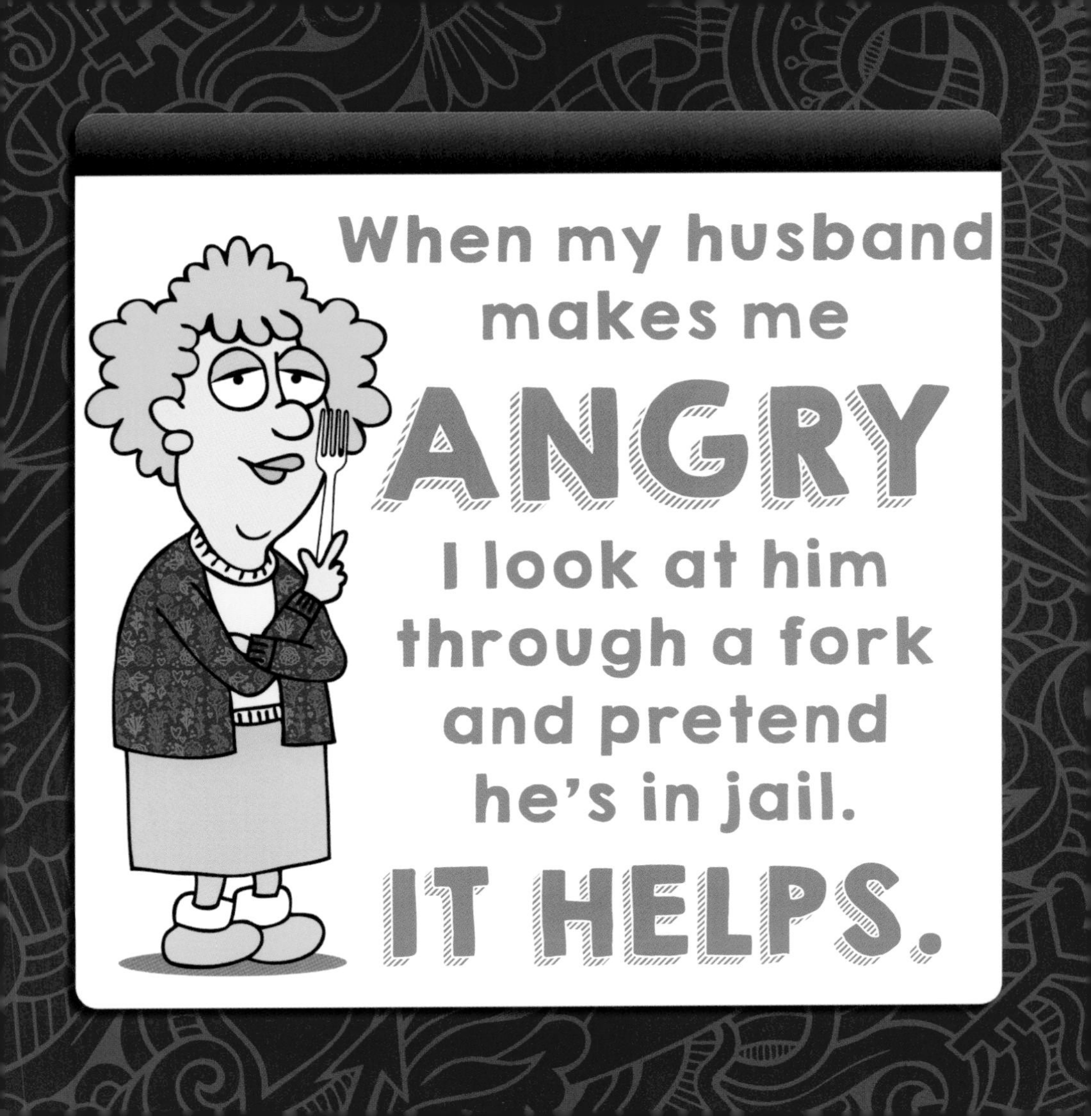

When my husband makes me

ANGRY

I look at him through a fork and pretend he's in jail.

IT HELPS.

PERFECT RELATIONSHIPS

ONLY EXIST IN:

- **THOUGHTS**
- **MOVIES**
- **FACEBOOK TIMELINES**

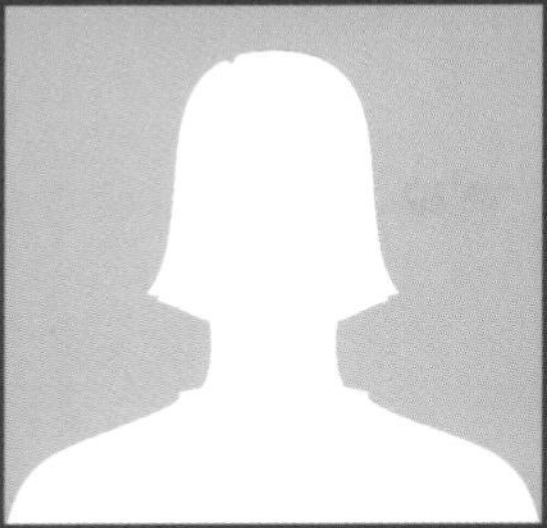

X

I don't mess with people with no

PROFILE PICTURE.

If you're scared of your own face...

SO AM I.

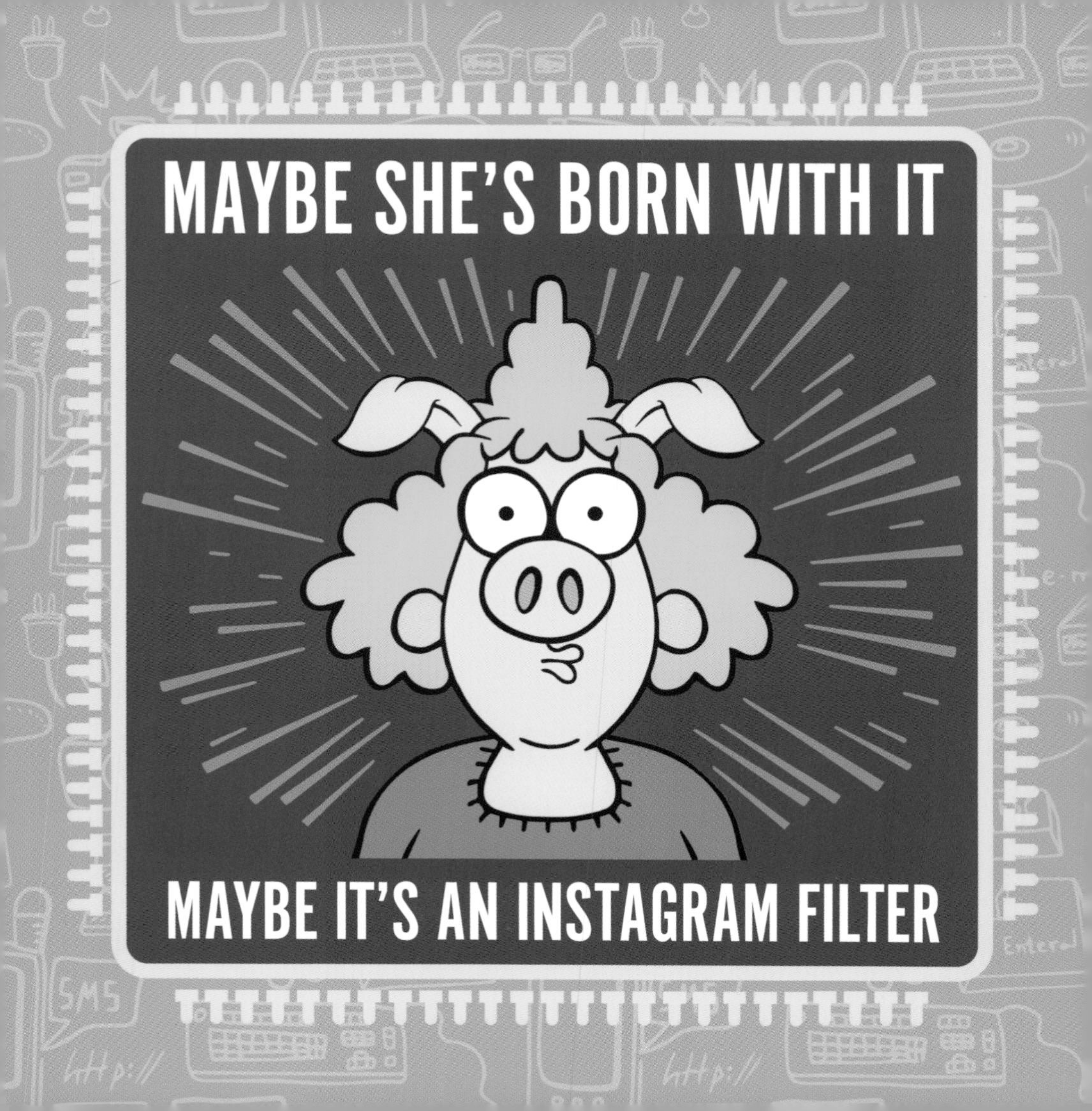
MAYBE SHE'S BORN WITH IT
MAYBE IT'S AN INSTAGRAM FILTER

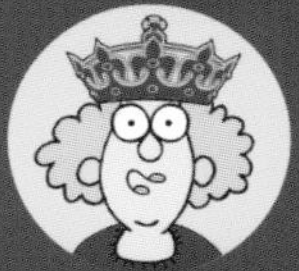

Have you heard of everyone's new favorite beauty product?

It's called a filter, although all it's done for me so far is to make me realize I look 100 times better as a freakin' cartoon PIG than I do as my actual real self.

How depressing!

And that's not the only time social media has got me into trouble. Turns out I'm not a Pinterest kind of woman—I'm more like an Amazon Prime kinda lady.

I've begged the postman to stop delivering my packages when my husband's home, but so far no luck.

The worst part of **ONLINE SHOPPING** is having to get up and go get your card out of your purse.

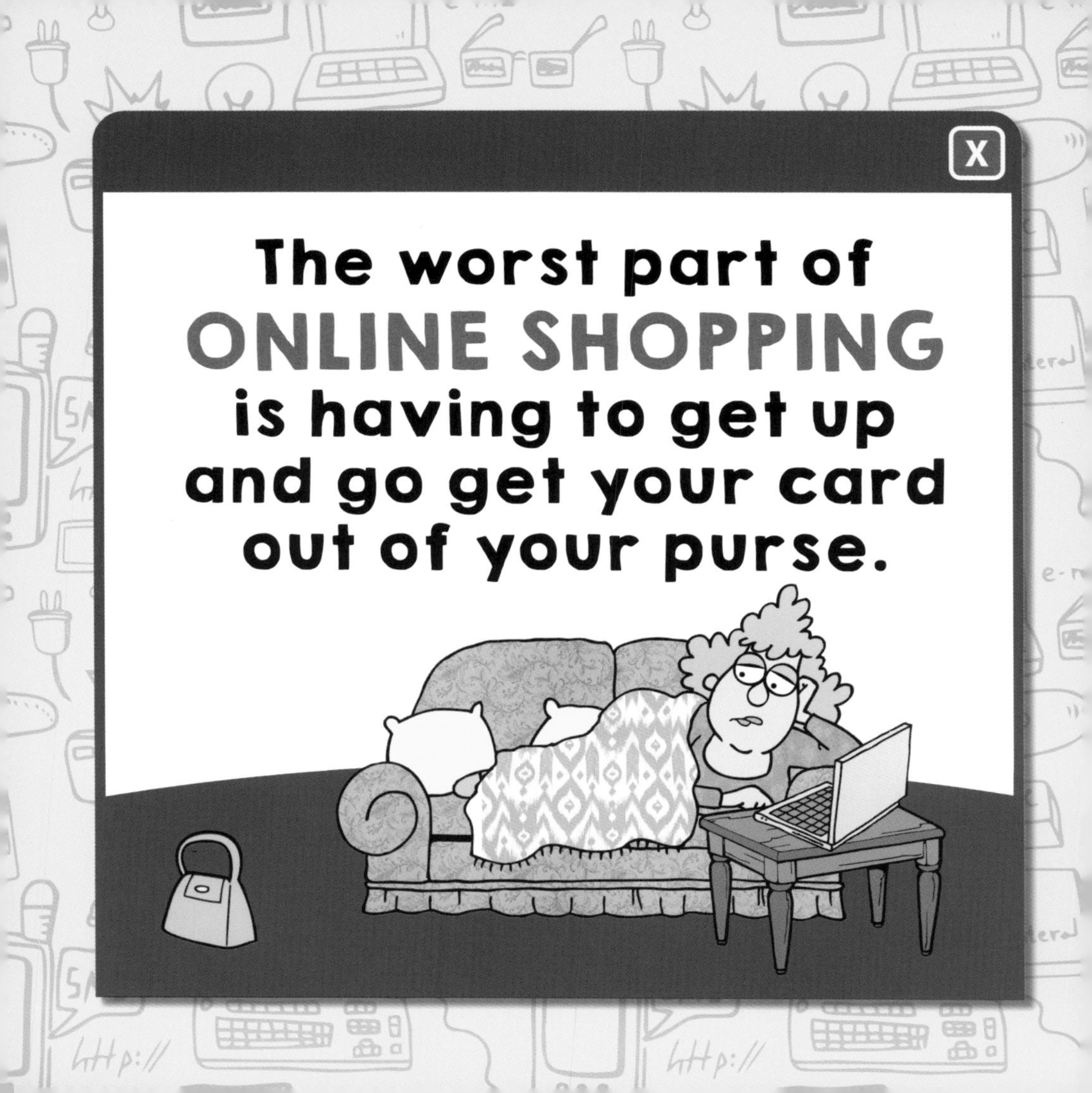

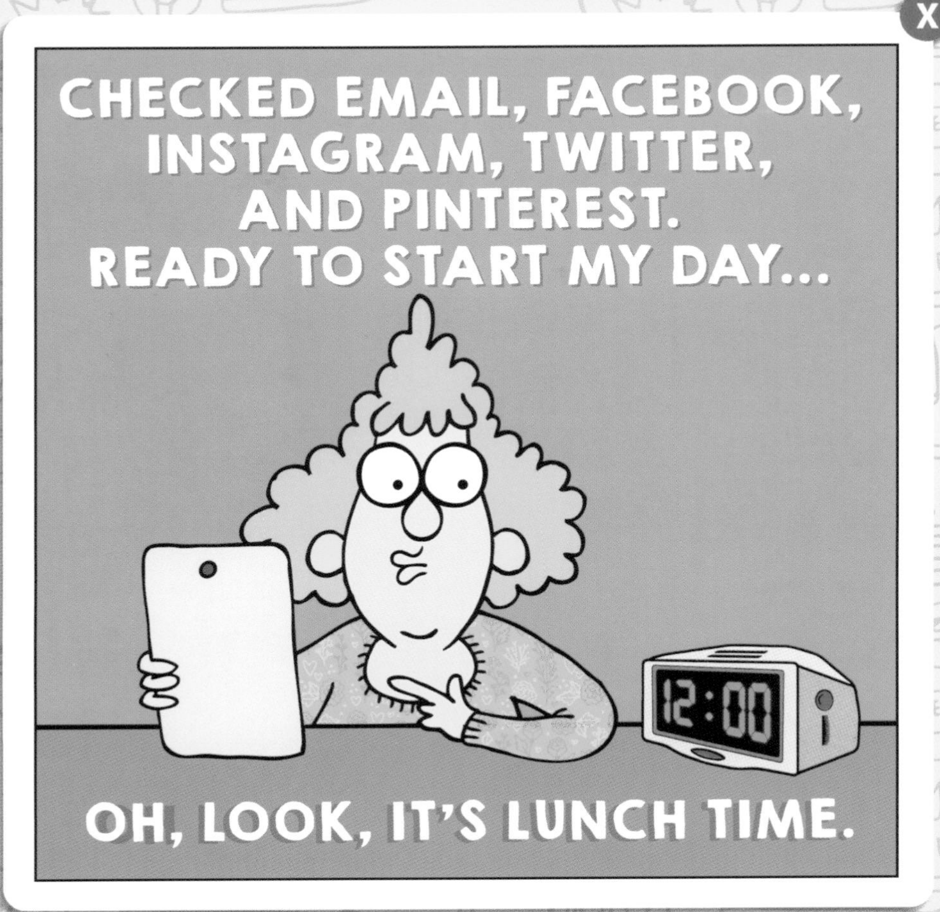
CHECKED EMAIL, FACEBOOK,
INSTAGRAM, TWITTER,
AND PINTEREST.
READY TO START MY DAY...
12:00
OH, LOOK, IT'S LUNCH TIME.

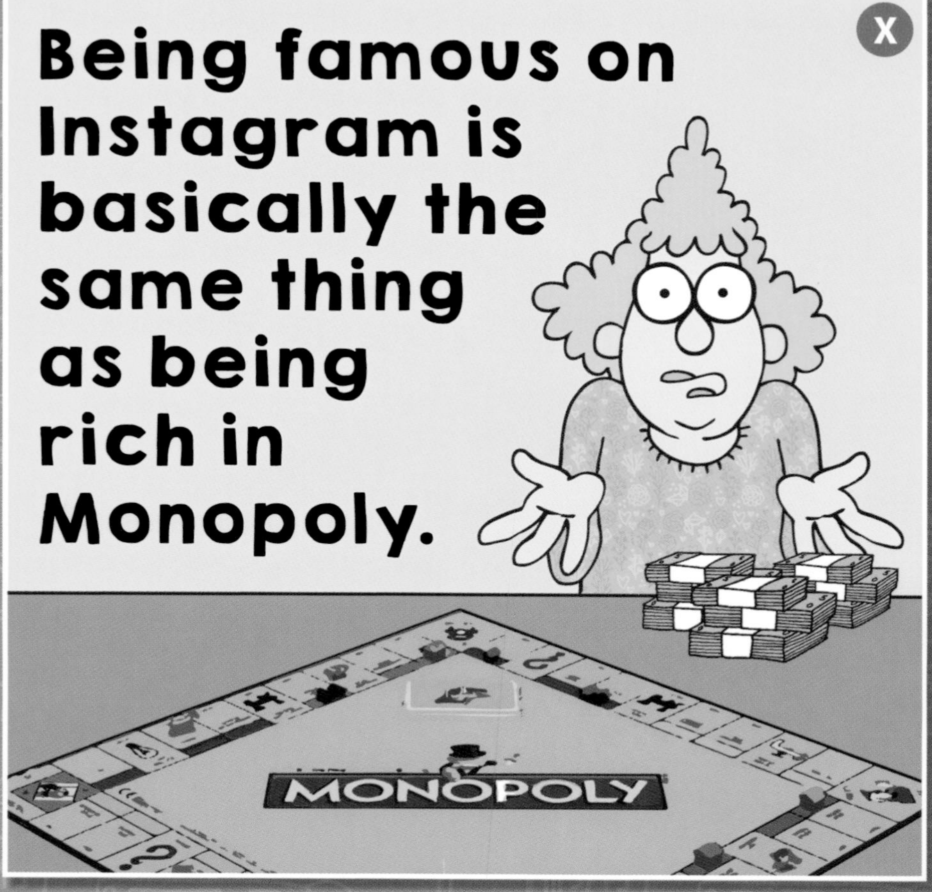
X
Being famous on Instagram is basically the same thing as being rich in Monopoly.
MONOPOLY

I haven't seen a new **KIM KARDASHIAN** selfie for 15 minutes...

SO I'VE CALLED THE COPS AND REPORTED HER MISSING.

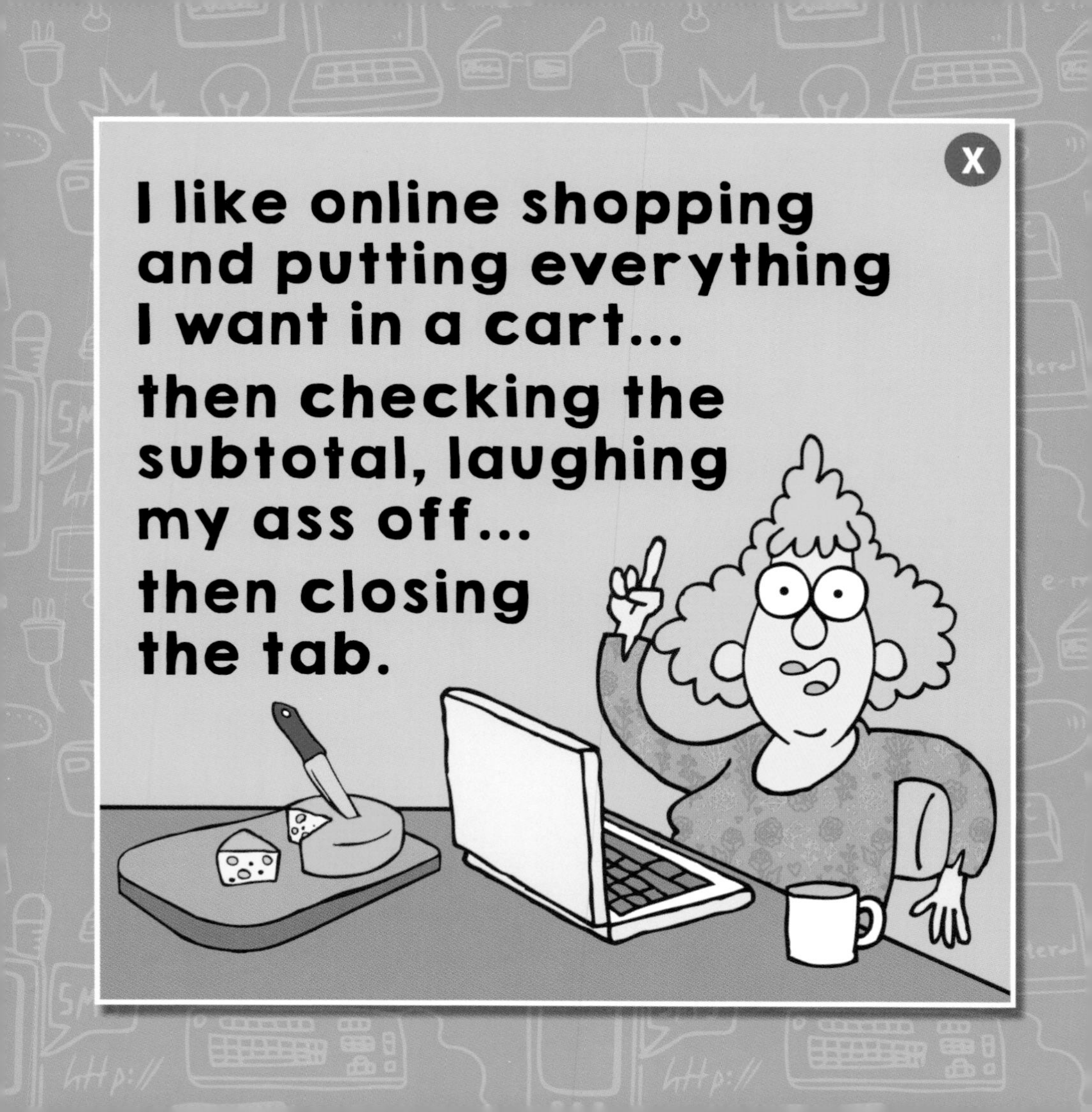
X
I like online shopping and putting everything I want in a cart... then checking the subtotal, laughing my ass off... then closing the tab.

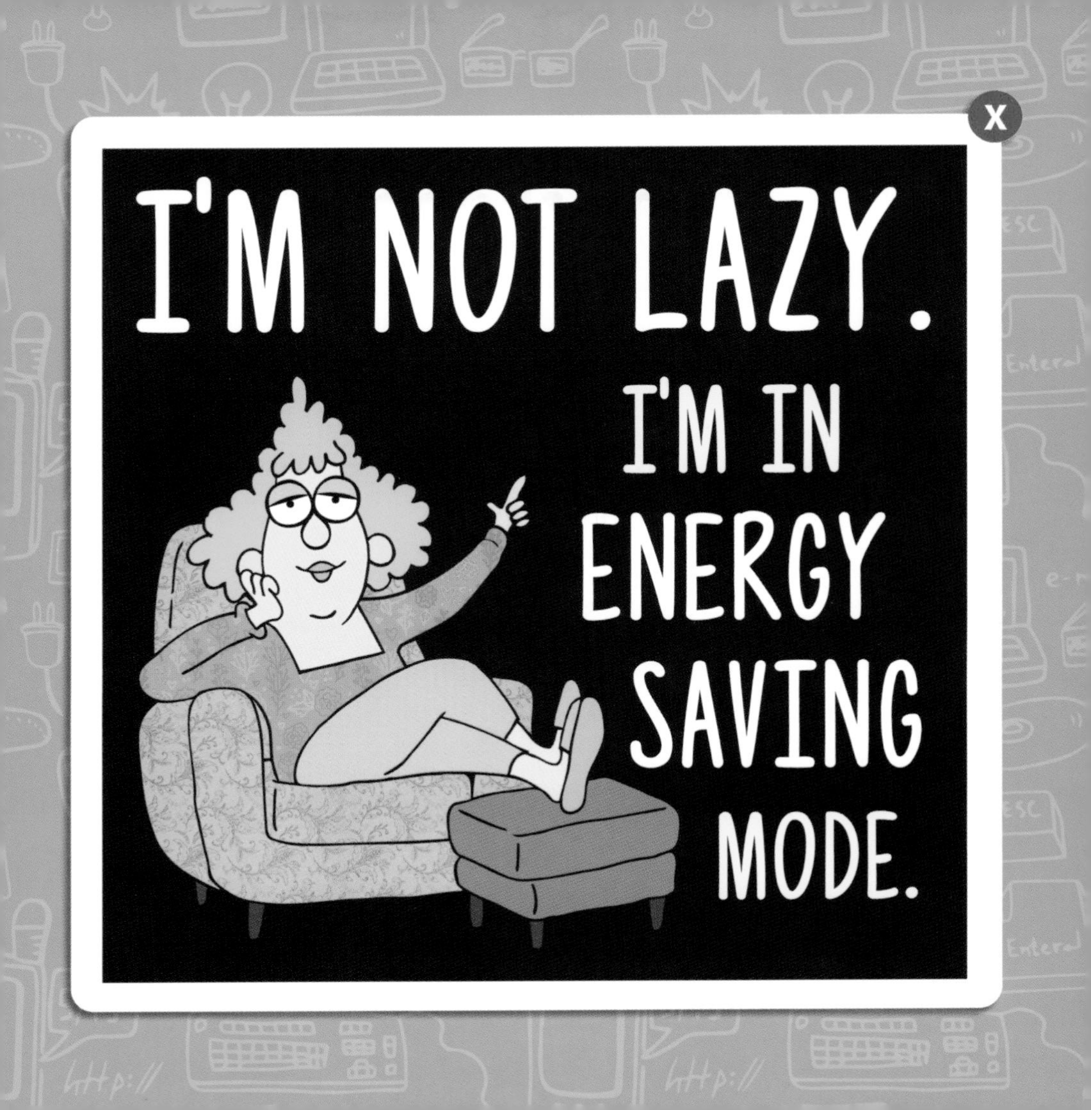

X
I'M NOT LAZY.
I'M IN ENERGY SAVING MODE.

⚠ FYI

⚠ **My phone is always on silent.**

⚠ **I don't even know if I have a ringtone.**

⚠ **If someone ever needs to contact me in an emergency, I suggest you call someone else.**

MY BRAIN IS LIKE MY INTERNET BROWSER:

SHOPPING
DINNER
WORK
CLEANING
KIDS

15 TABS ARE OPEN, 3 OF THEM ARE FROZEN, AND I HAVE NO IDEA WHERE THAT MUSIC IS COMING FROM!

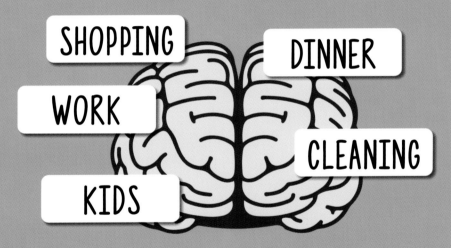

I normally mind my own business, but if someone is arguing on Facebook, I'm reading all 694 comments.

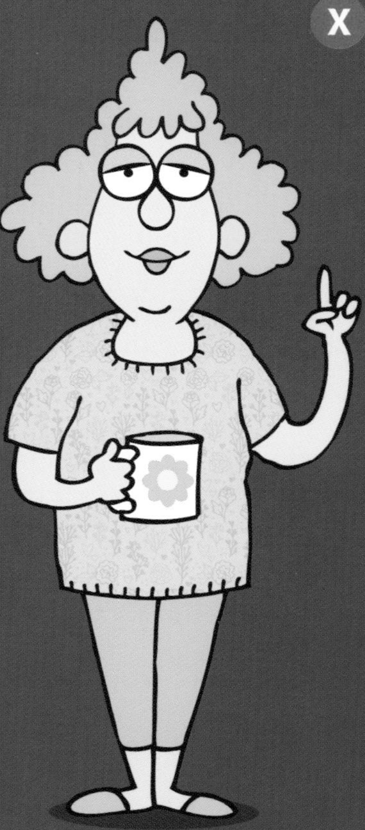

⚠ ONLINE SHOPPING

BECAUSE IT'S FROWNED UPON TO BE IN A STORE WITH NO BRA, DIRTY HAIR, AND A GLASS OF WINE.

HAVE YOU EVER GIVEN THE FINGER TO A TEXT MESSAGE, OR IS THAT JUST ME?

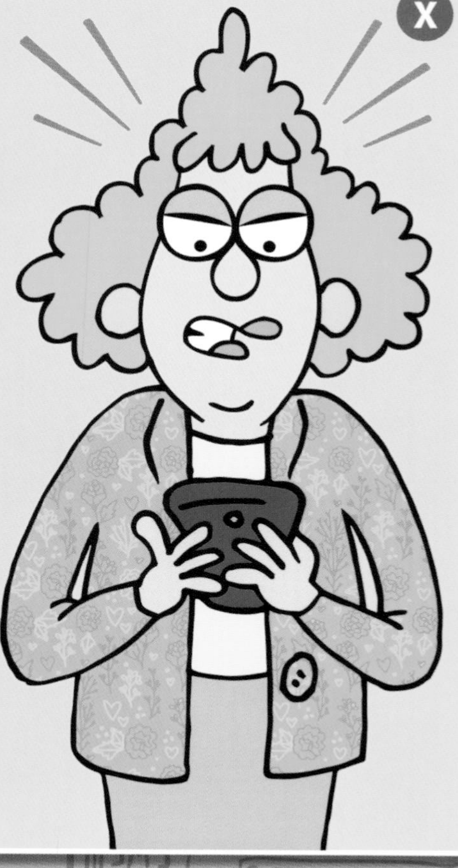

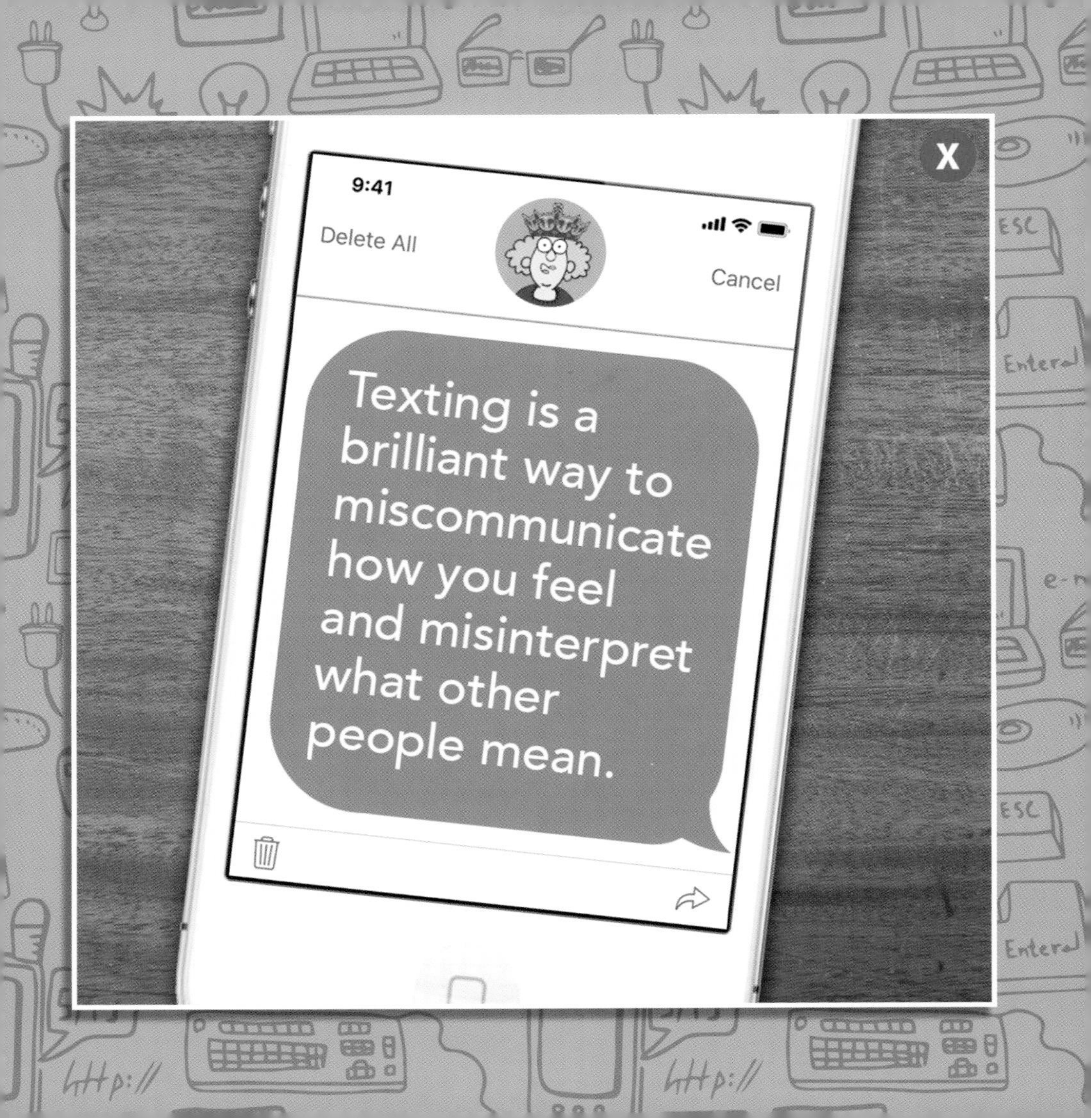
9:41
Delete All
Cancel
Texting is a brilliant way to miscommunicate how you feel and misinterpret what other people mean.

When you're busy bragging on Facebook, remember there are people who know you in real life.

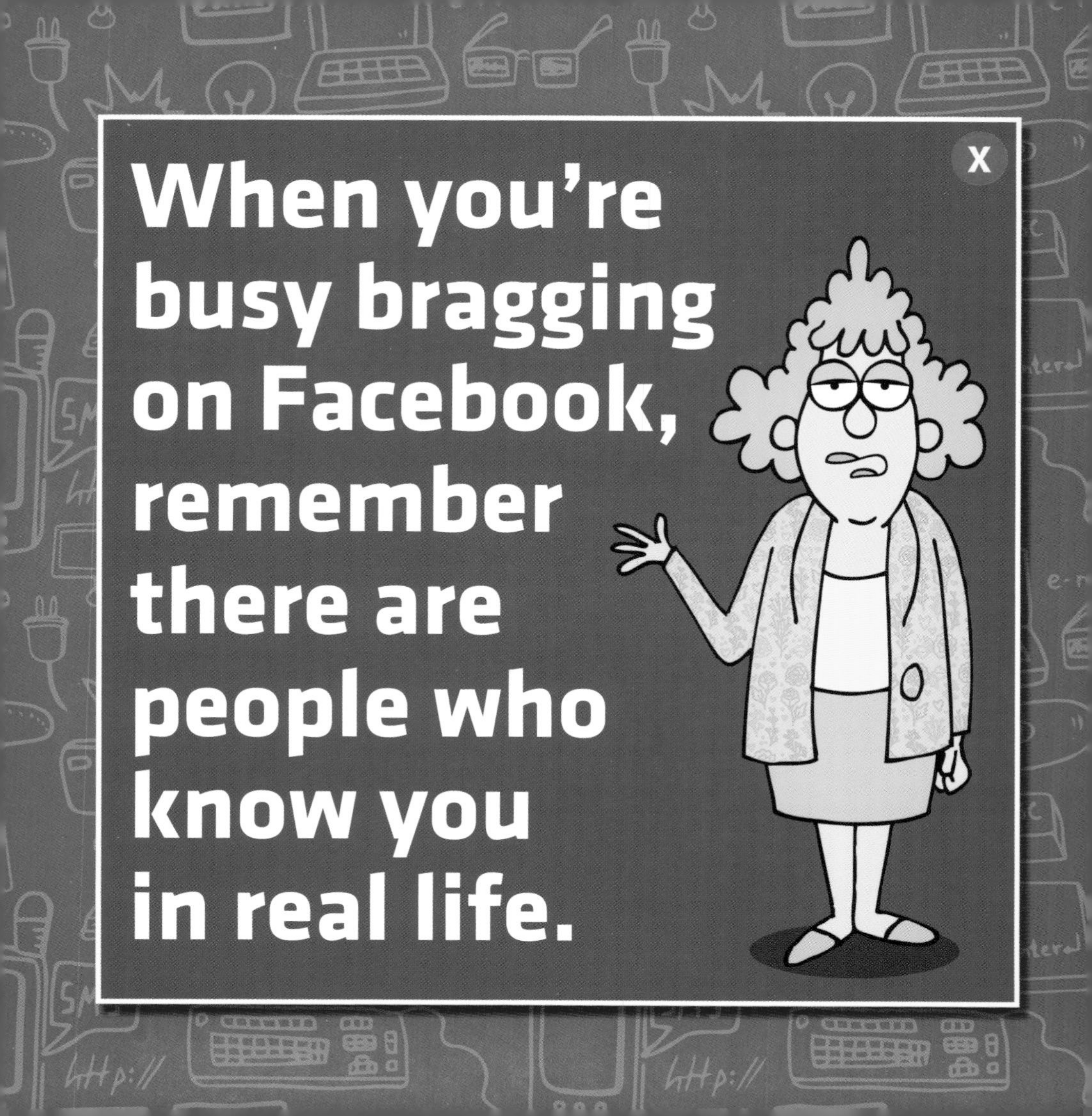

OK, I CONFESS

I keep some people's numbers in my phone just so I know not to answer when they call.

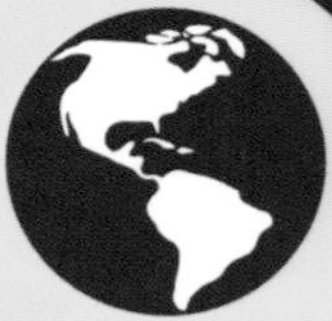

This is a sponsored post

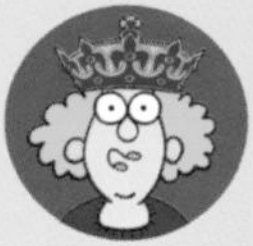

ONLY KIDDING!

There are a whole bunch of cool ways to make money on the internet these days though folks. I make a killin' selling Walt's old socks on Ebay–people are using them to deter people sitting next to them on public transport–clever, huh?

You can also make BIG BUCKS being an "influencer." All you have to be is attractive, fashionable, young, and cool–so that's me out. I am an influence in other ways though, usually a freakin' BAD ONE.

YES OF COURSE I'M ATHLETIC. I SURF THE INTERNET EVERY DAY.

If I block you on **SOCIAL MEDIA** the block applies to **REAL LIFE.**

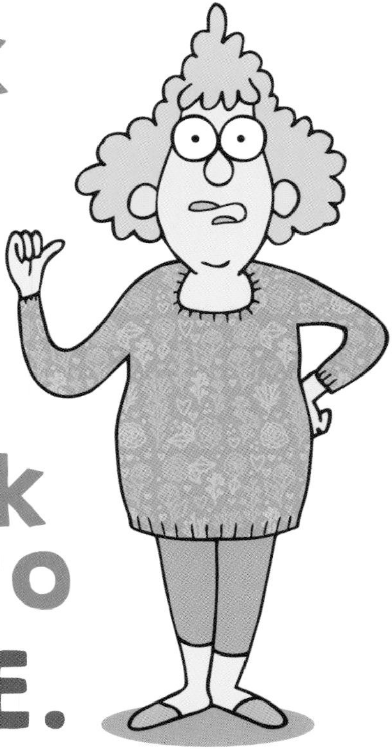

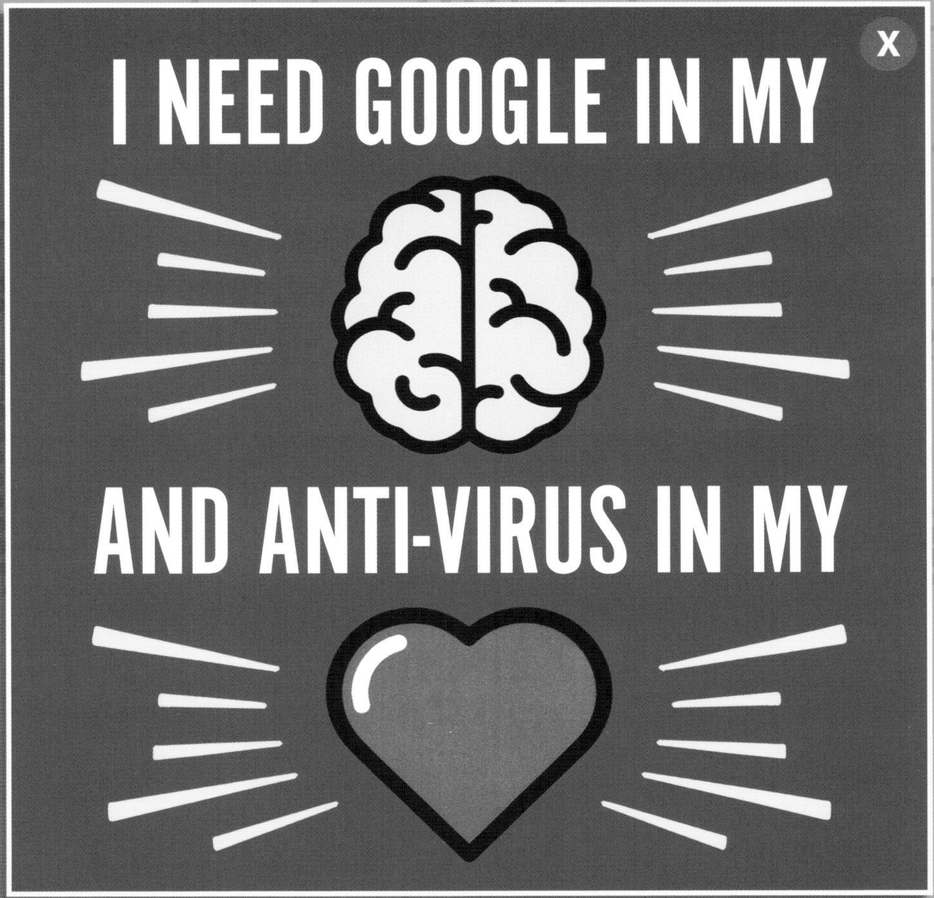
X
I NEED GOOGLE IN MY
AND ANTI-VIRUS IN MY

SORRY...

I've got my NETFLIX pants on,

so I'm in for the night!

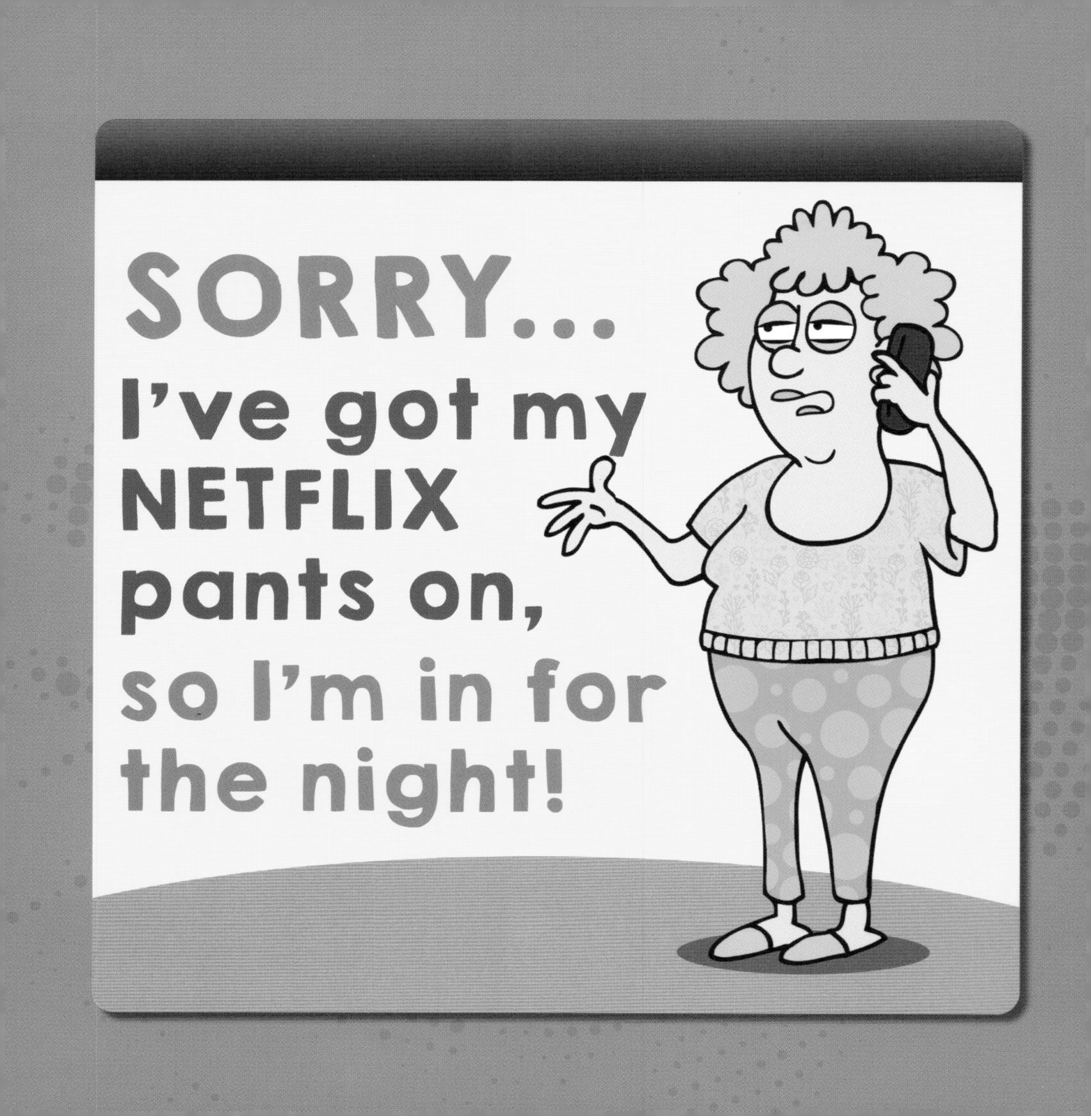

LEGGINGS WERE ONCE A GIRL'S BEST FRIEND. THEN SNAPCHAT FILTERS CAME ALONG.

UNLESS YOUR NAME IS

Google

STOP ACTING
LIKE YOU
KNOW
EVERYTHING!

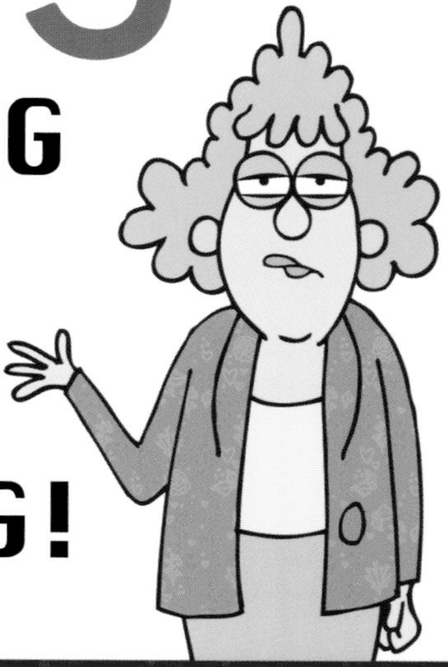

“The trouble with quotes on the internet is that you never know if they are genuine.”

- Albert Einstein

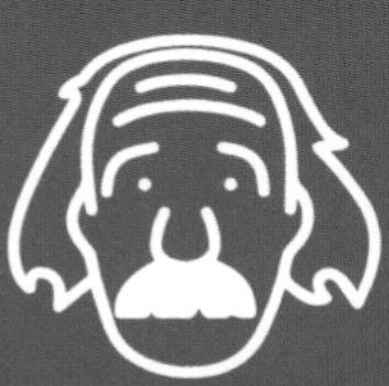

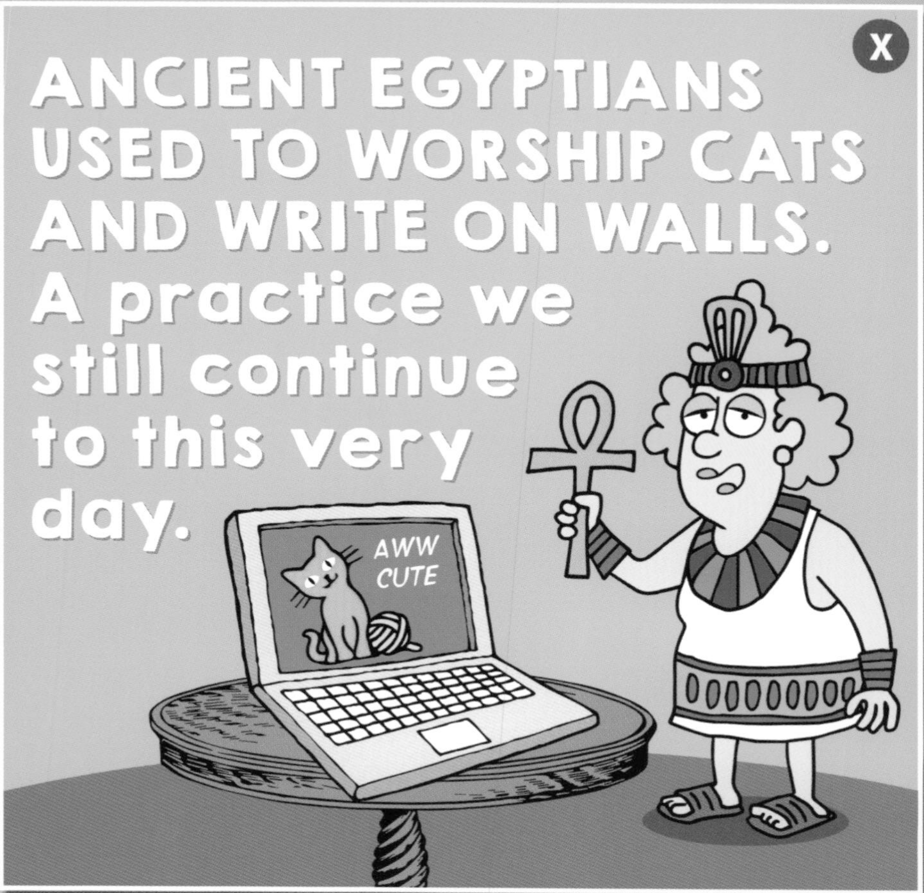

X
ANCIENT EGYPTIANS USED TO WORSHIP CATS AND WRITE ON WALLS.
A practice we still continue to this very day.
AWW CUTE

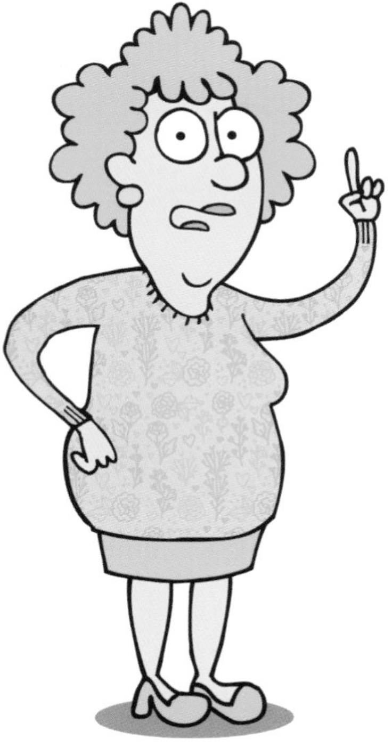

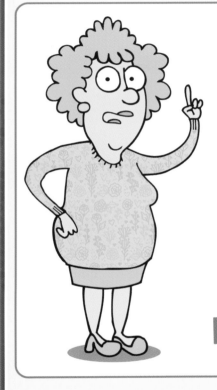

If I'm not online for more than two days, CALL THE POLICE I've been kidnapped.

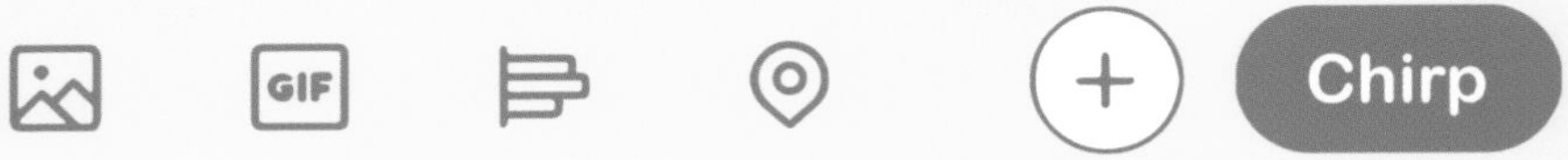
GIF
Chirp

BEING POPULAR ON THE INTERNET IS LIKE SITTING AT THE COOL TABLE IN A MENTAL HOSPITAL.

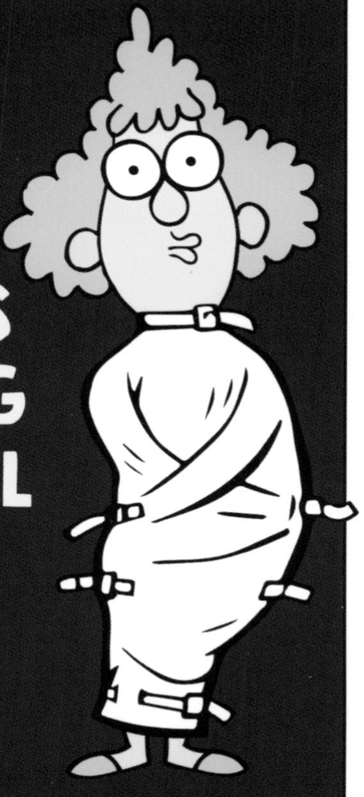

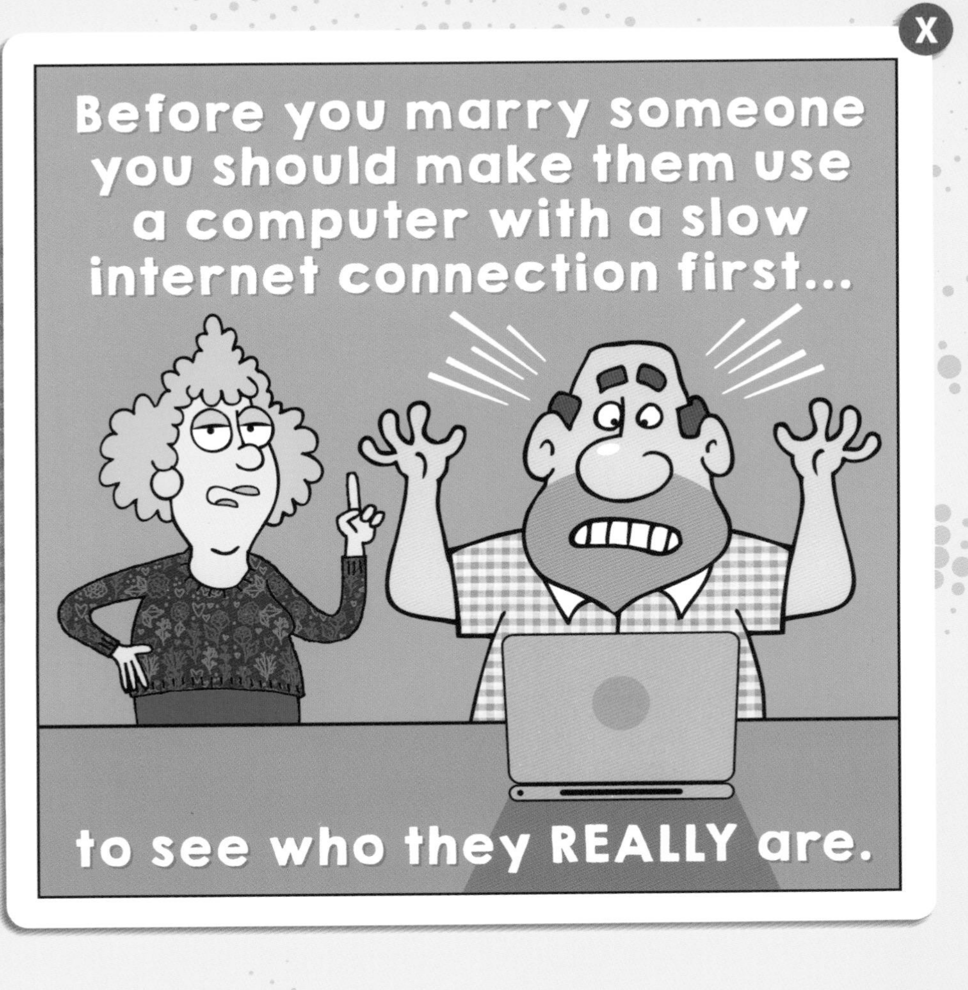
Before you marry someone you should make them use a computer with a slow internet connection first...
to see who they REALLY are.

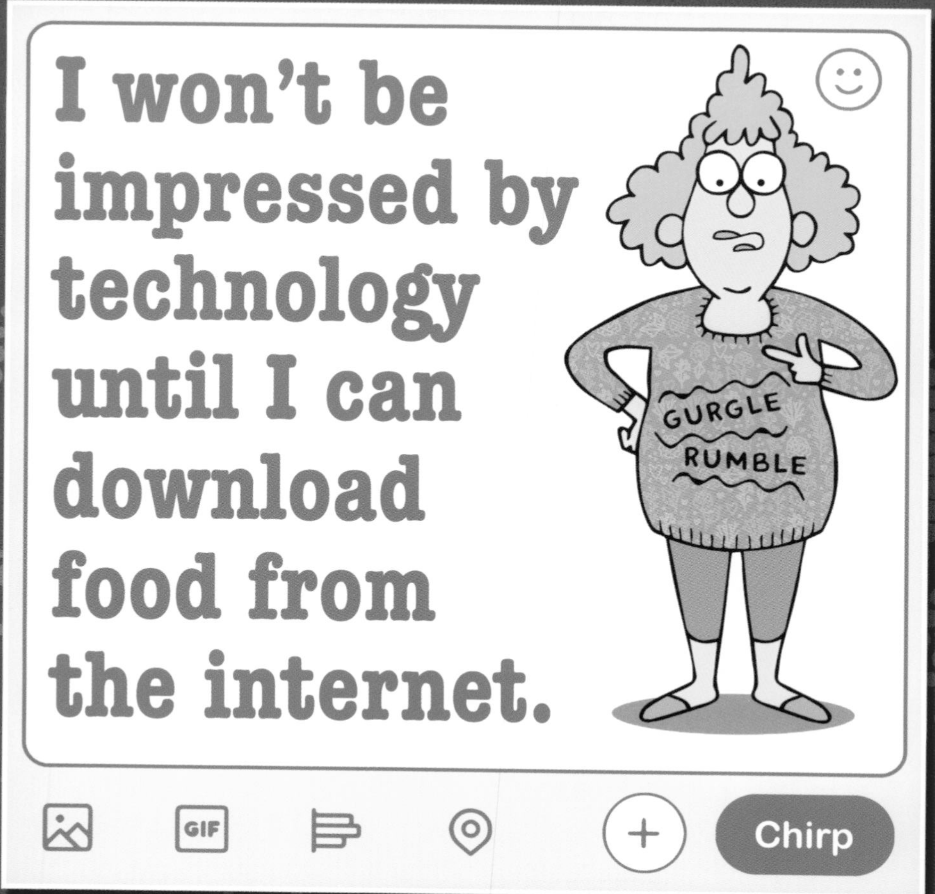
I won't be impressed by technology until I can download food from the internet.
GURGLE
RUMBLE
GIF
Chirp

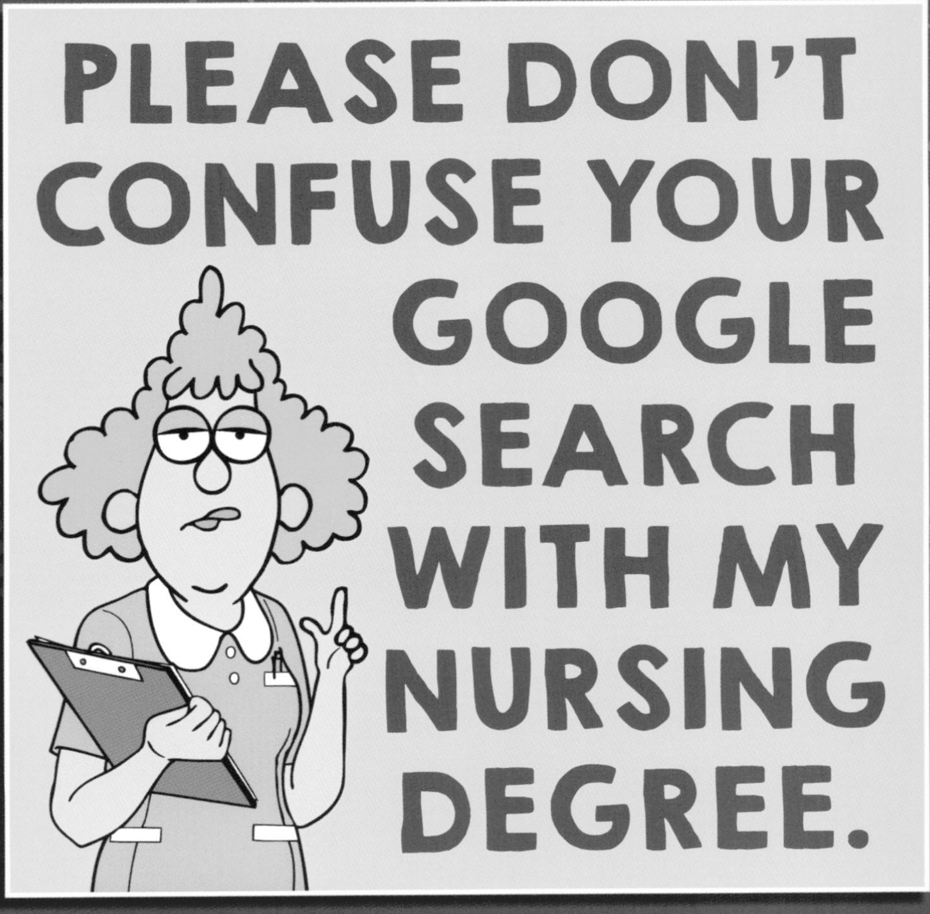
PLEASE DON'T CONFUSE YOUR GOOGLE SEARCH WITH MY NURSING DEGREE.

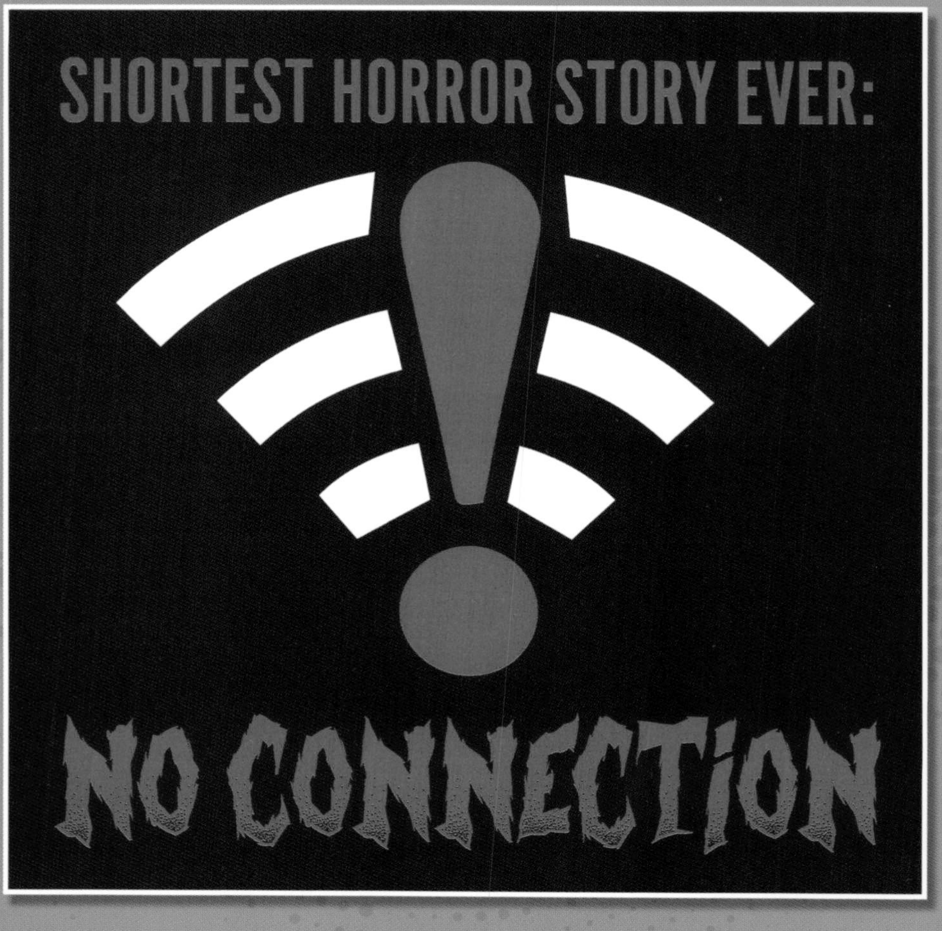
SHORTEST HORROR STORY EVER:
NO CONNECTION

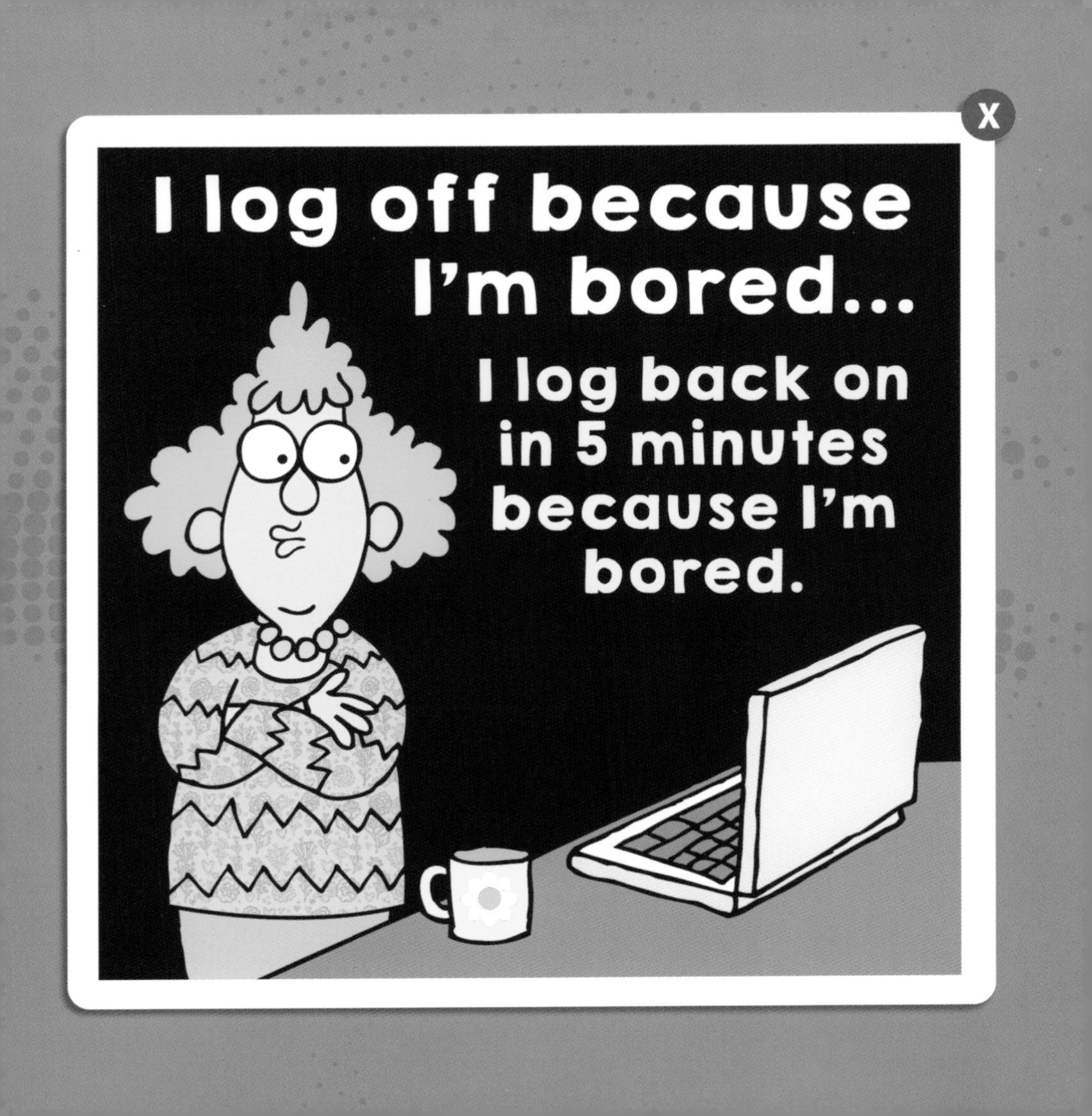
I log off because I'm bored...
I log back on in 5 minutes because I'm bored.
X

The best thing about being

OVER 40

is that we did all our stupid stuff before the invention of the internet.

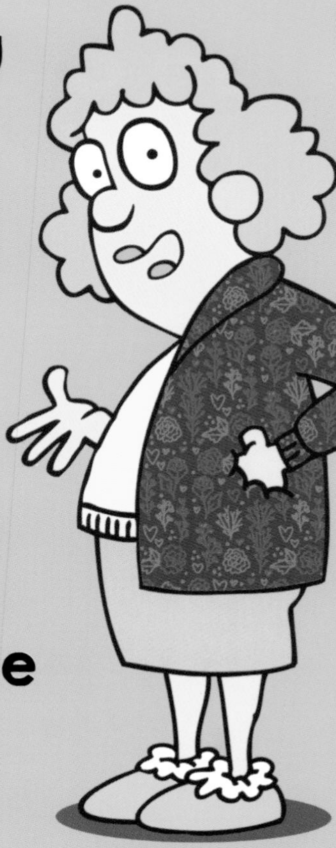

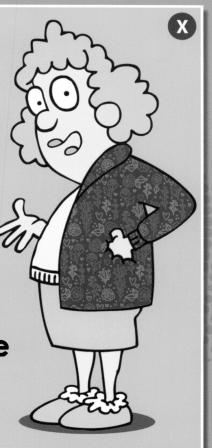

THANKS TO INSTAGRAM I NOW KNOW WHAT EVERYONE'S BATHROOM MIRROR LOOKS LIKE

Social media is like a

REFRIGERATOR.

You know there's nothing new inside but you still check it out every ten minutes.

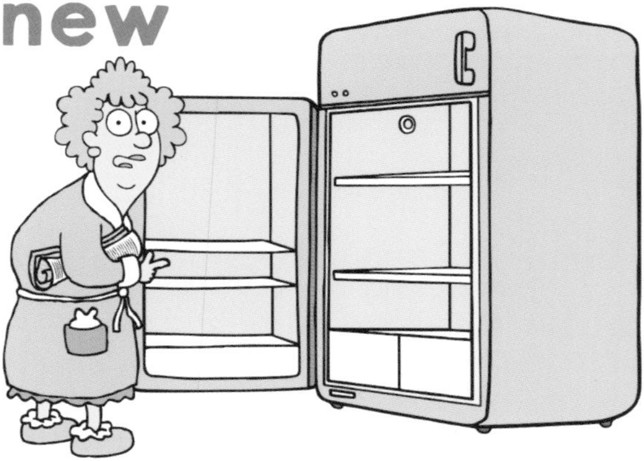

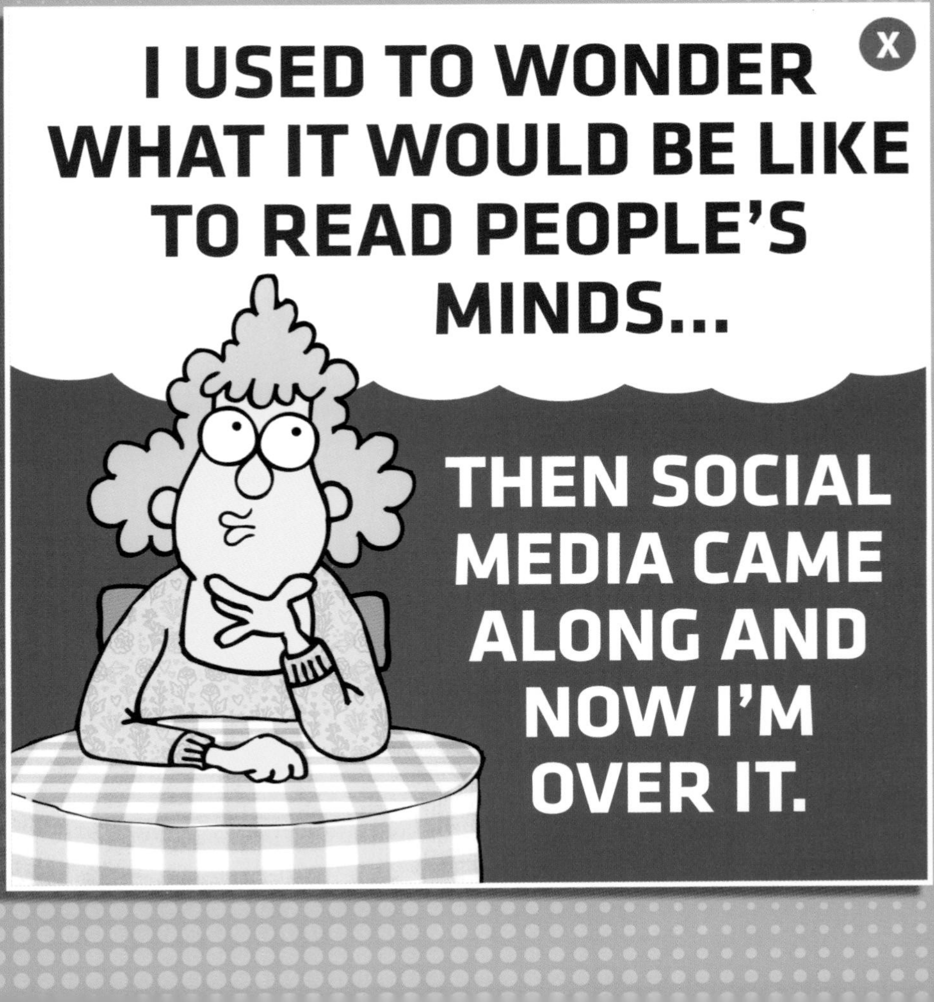
I USED TO WONDER WHAT IT WOULD BE LIKE TO READ PEOPLE'S MINDS...
THEN SOCIAL MEDIA CAME ALONG AND NOW I'M OVER IT.

QUTTING FACEBOOK IS THE NEW RUNNING AWAY FROM HOME.

We all know you're doing it for attention, and we all know you're coming back!

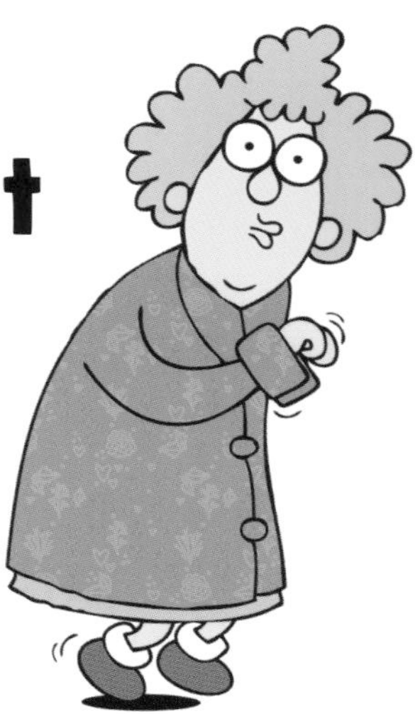

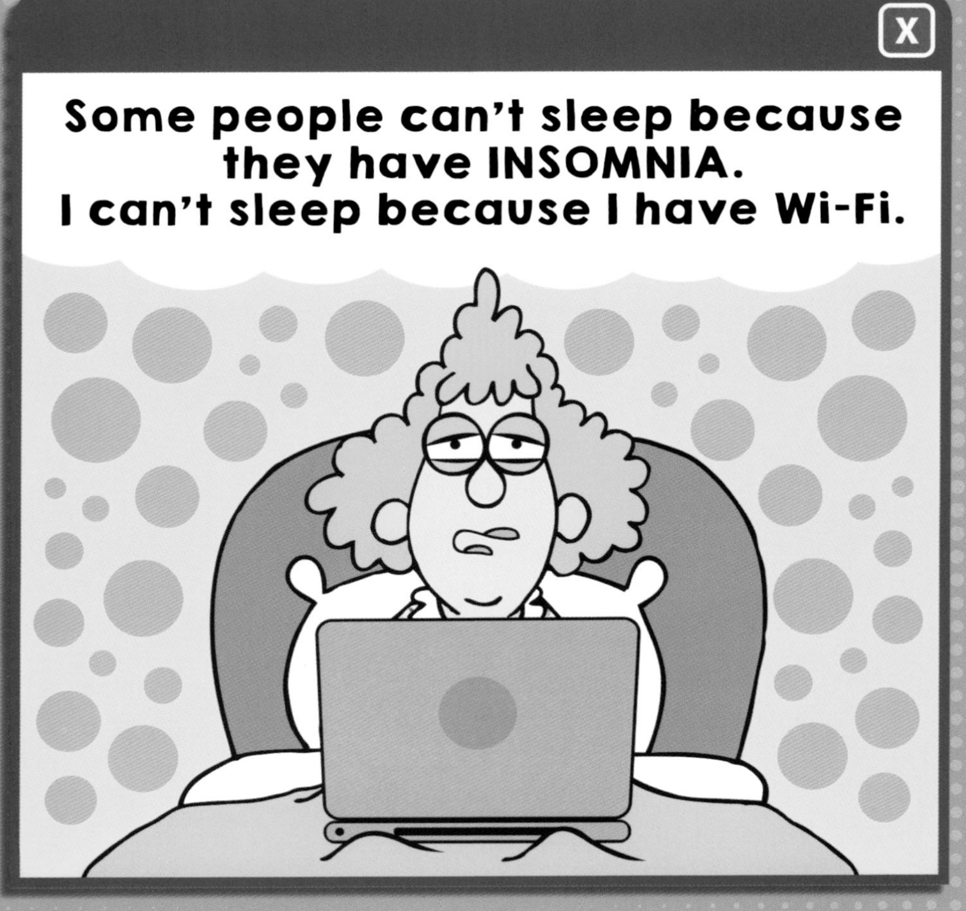
X
Some people can't sleep because they have INSOMNIA.
I can't sleep because I have Wi-Fi.

I'm changing my name to "NOBODY" on Instagram.

That way, when I see a stupid post, I'll like it and it will say "NOBODY LIKES THIS POST."

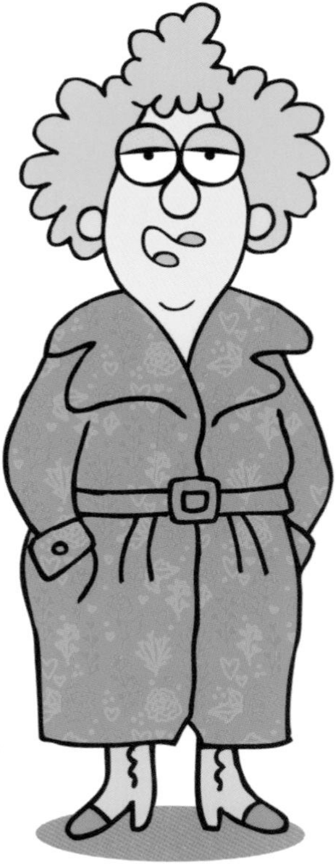

I walked into the kitchen asking my daughter for a phone book. She just laughed, said I was old, then passed me her phone instead. Long story short...

Spider dead, phone broke, and daughter crying in her room.

CAUTION

I HAVE NO FILTER.

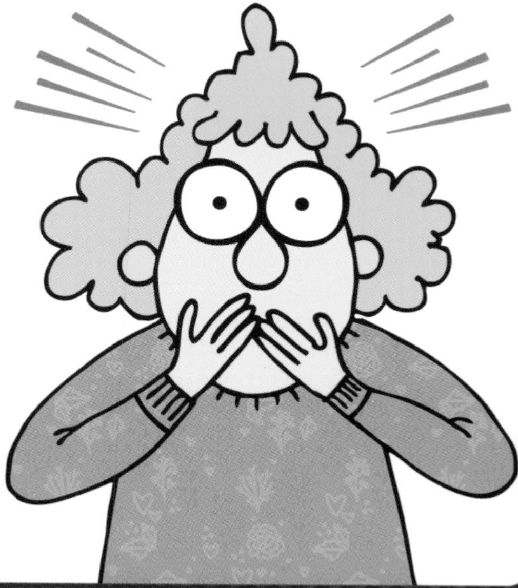

" Yes, you should definitely post that status. Everyone will think it's soooo funny. **"** -Wine

STALKING

is such a strong word.

Let's call it **SOCIAL RESEARCH** instead.

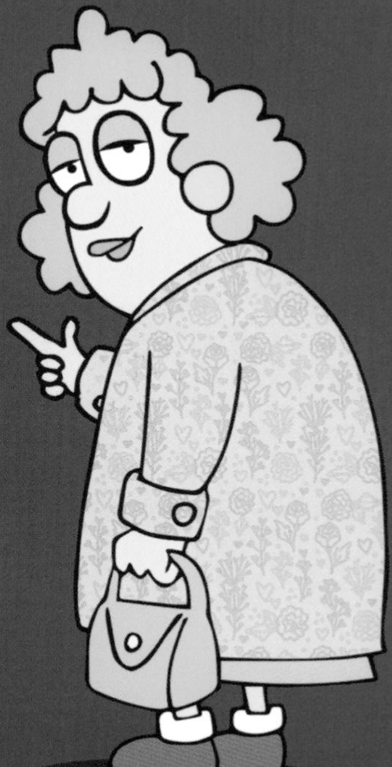

DON'T KNOW WHERE YOUR KIDS ARE?

Turn off the internet and they'll show up quickly enough!

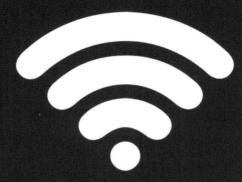

FYI

LIKING YOUR OWN FACEBOOK STATUS IS LIKE GIVING YOURSELF A HIGH FIVE IN PUBLIC.

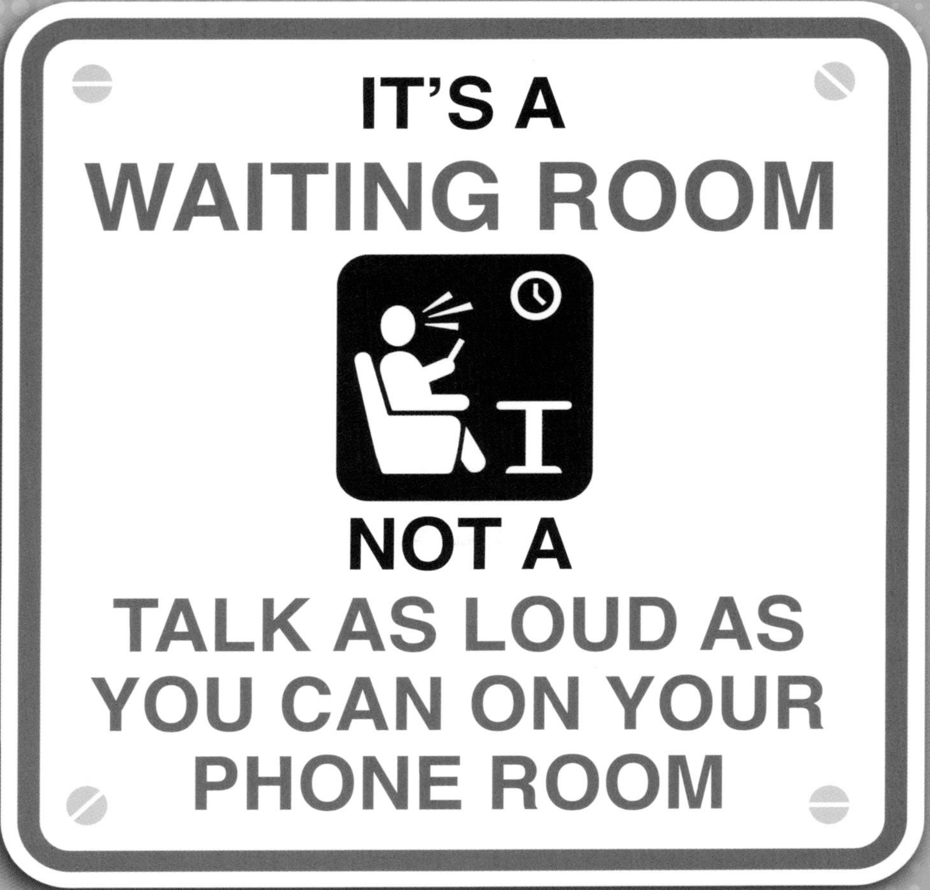
IT'S A
WAITING ROOM
NOT A
TALK AS LOUD AS
YOU CAN ON YOUR
PHONE ROOM

Me and my husband like to

PARTY

And by party I mean...
put on Netflix
and try to
stay awake
for half an
hour.

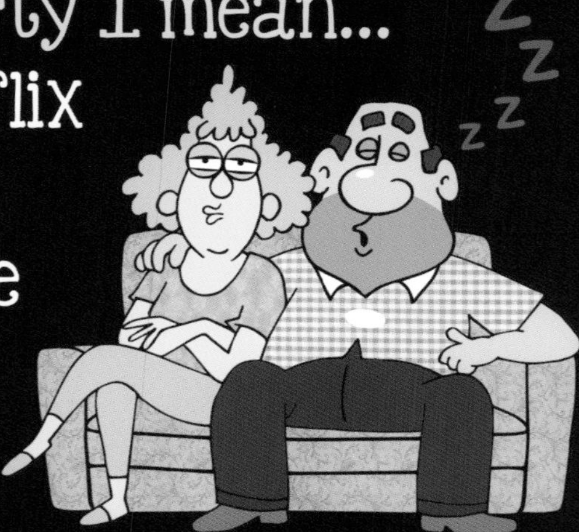

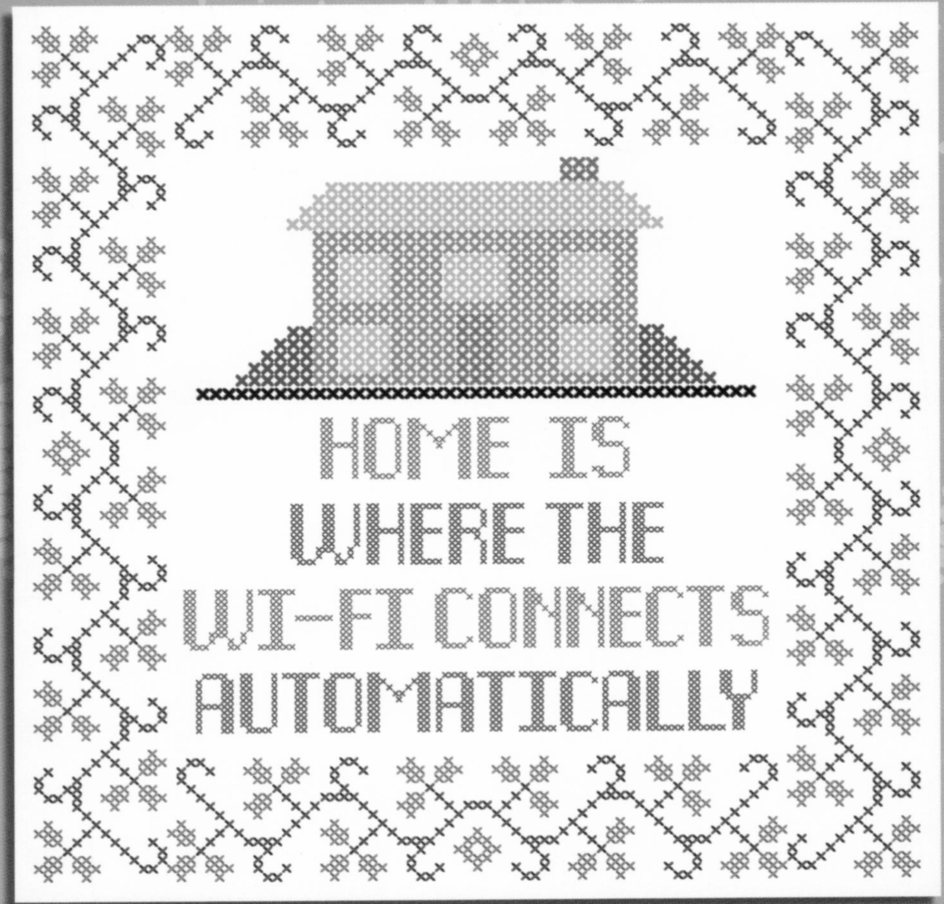
HOME IS
WHERE THE
WI-FI CONNECTS
AUTOMATICALLY

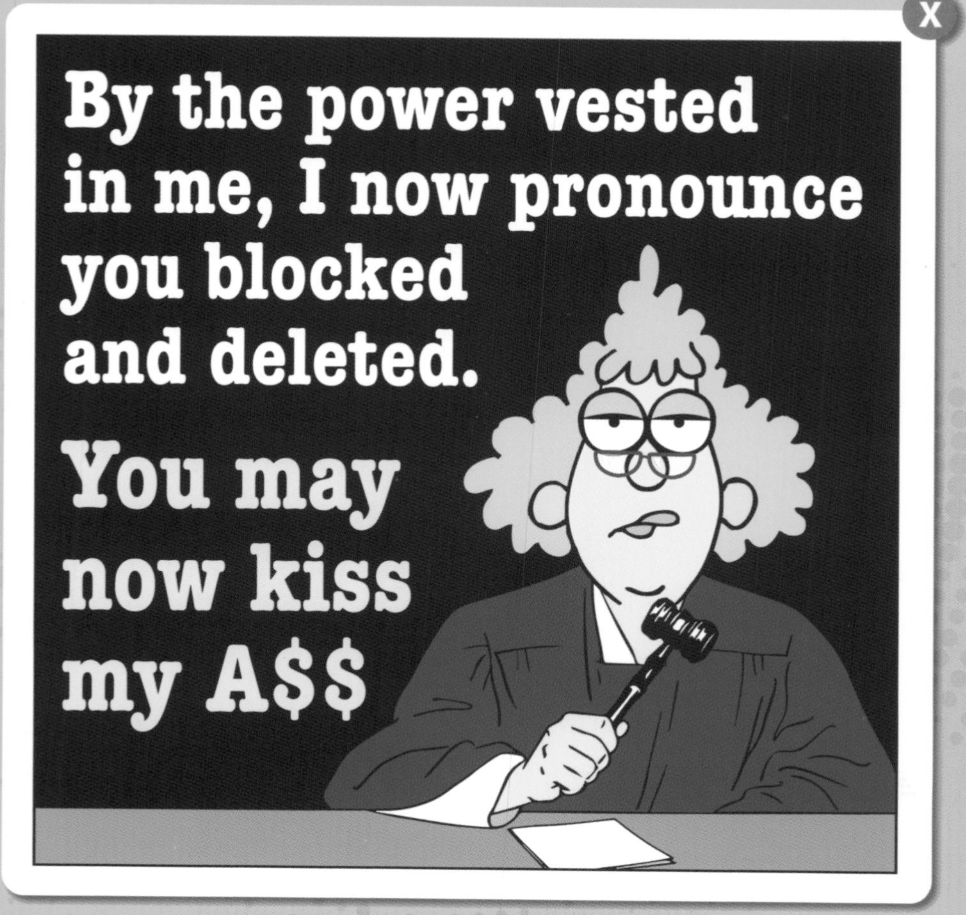
By the power vested in me, I now pronounce you blocked and deleted.
You may now kiss my A$$

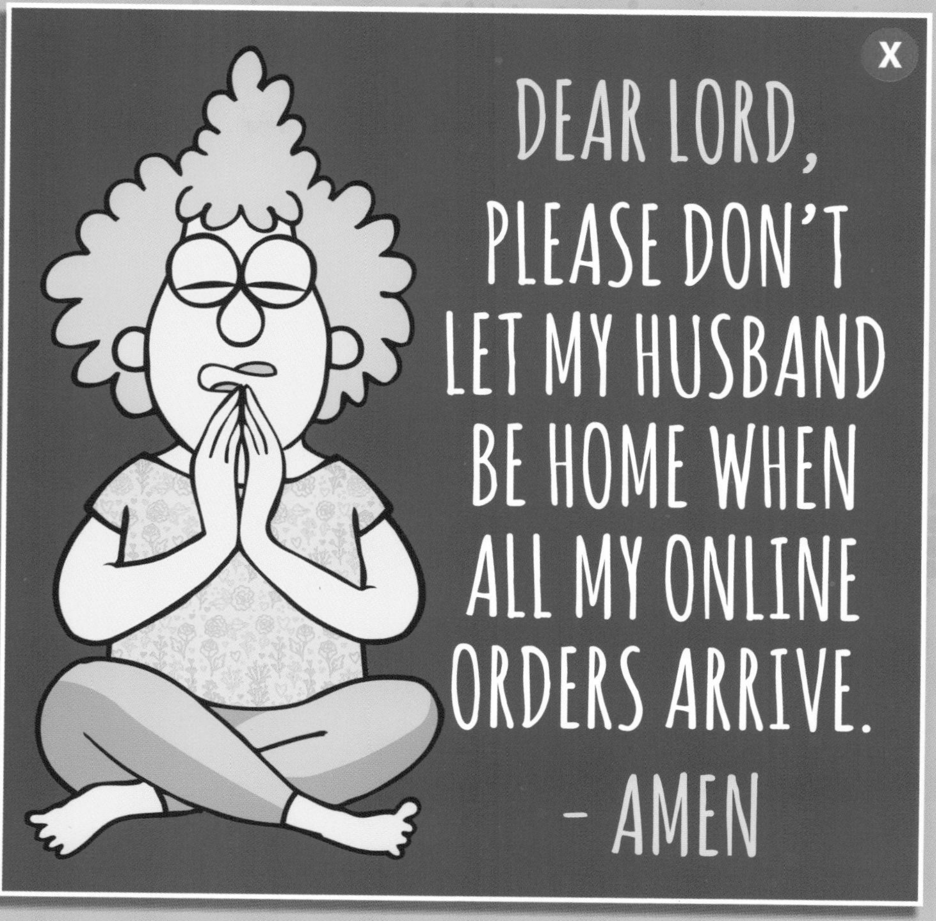
X
DEAR LORD,
PLEASE DON'T
LET MY HUSBAND
BE HOME WHEN
ALL MY ONLINE
ORDERS ARRIVE.
- AMEN

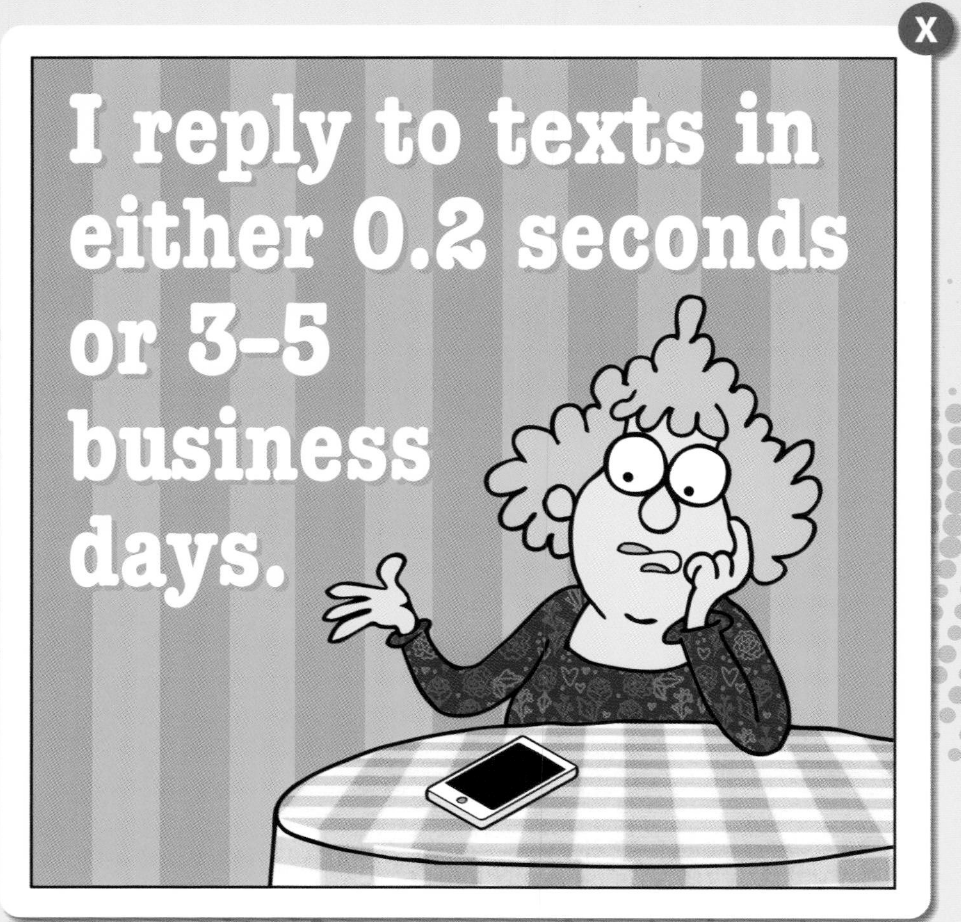
I reply to texts in either 0.2 seconds or 3–5 business days.
X

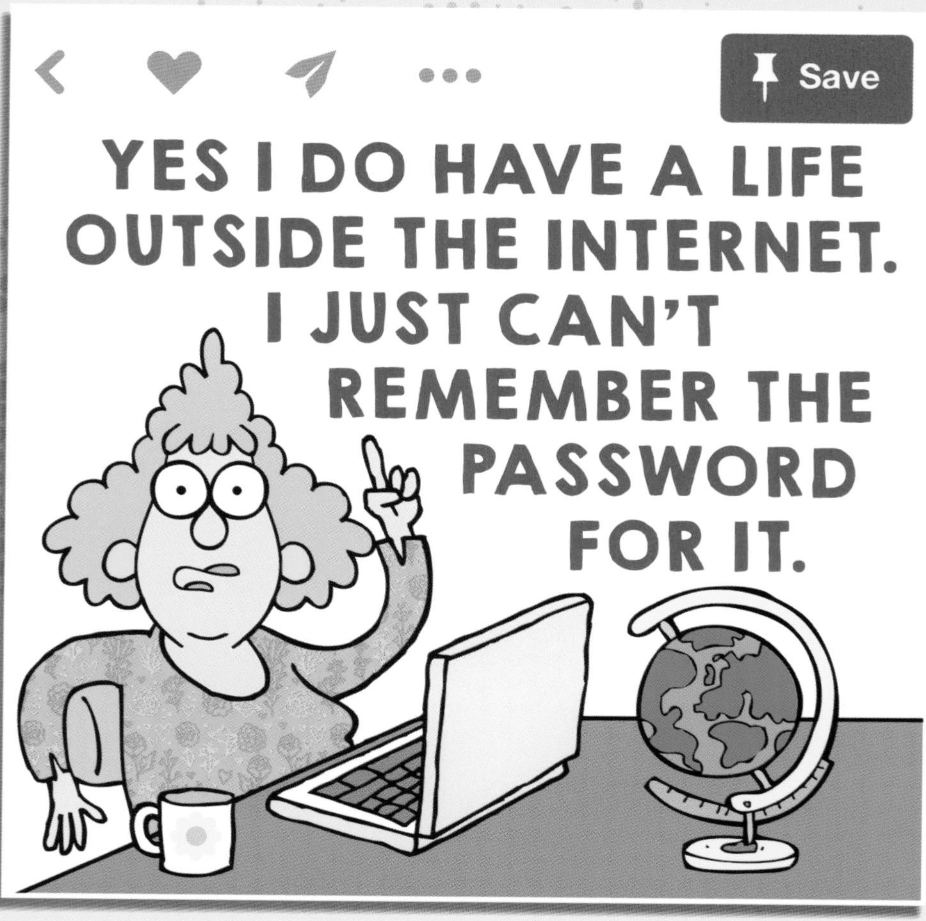
Save
YES I DO HAVE A LIFE OUTSIDE THE INTERNET. I JUST CAN'T REMEMBER THE PASSWORD FOR IT.

Santa saw your **Facebook** posts...

You're getting a dictionary this year.

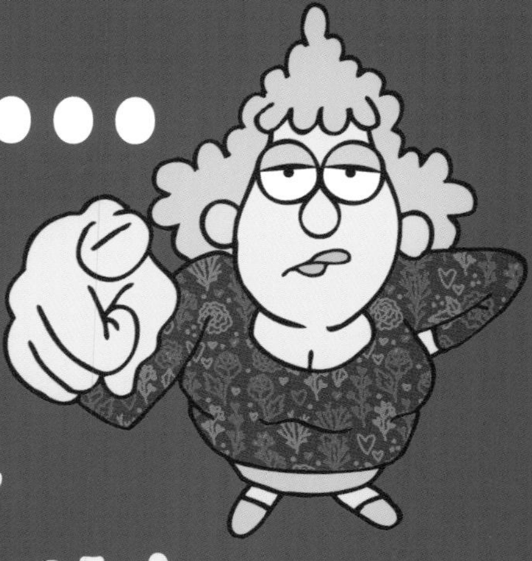

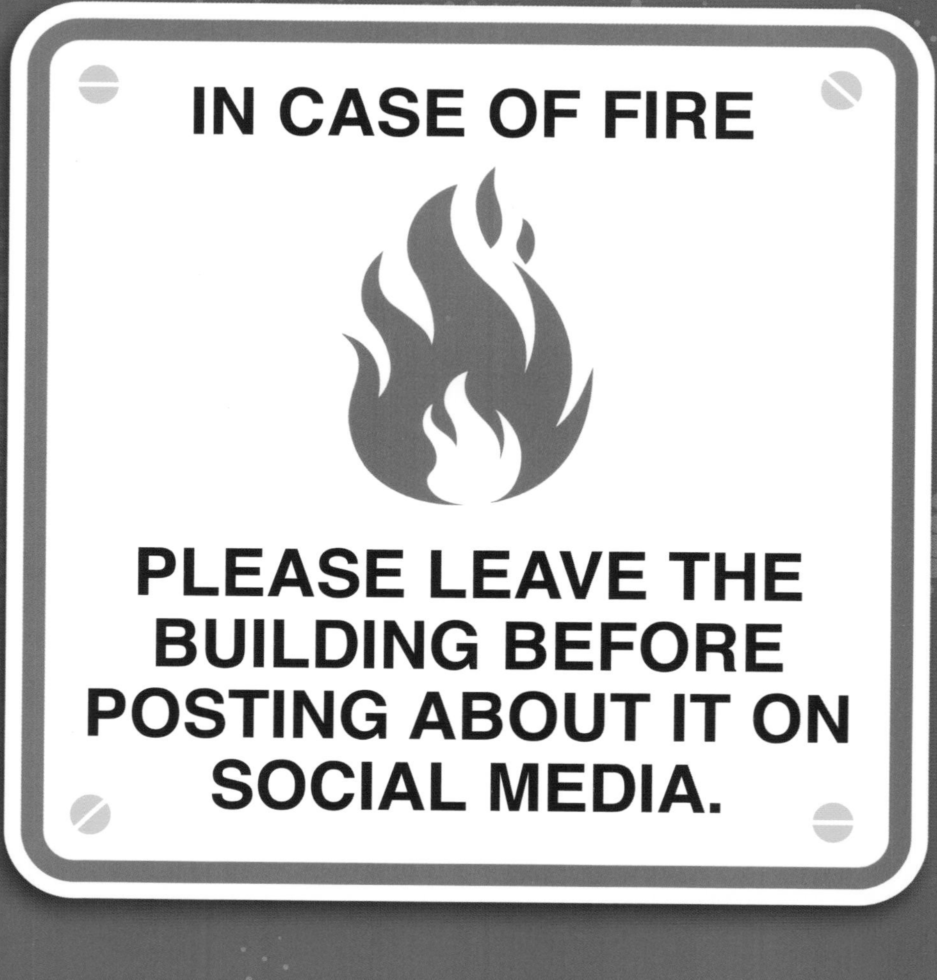
IN CASE OF FIRE
PLEASE LEAVE THE BUILDING BEFORE POSTING ABOUT IT ON SOCIAL MEDIA.

No matter how nice your pictures are or how real your quotes may be, there are some people who will never hit the like button just because it's you.

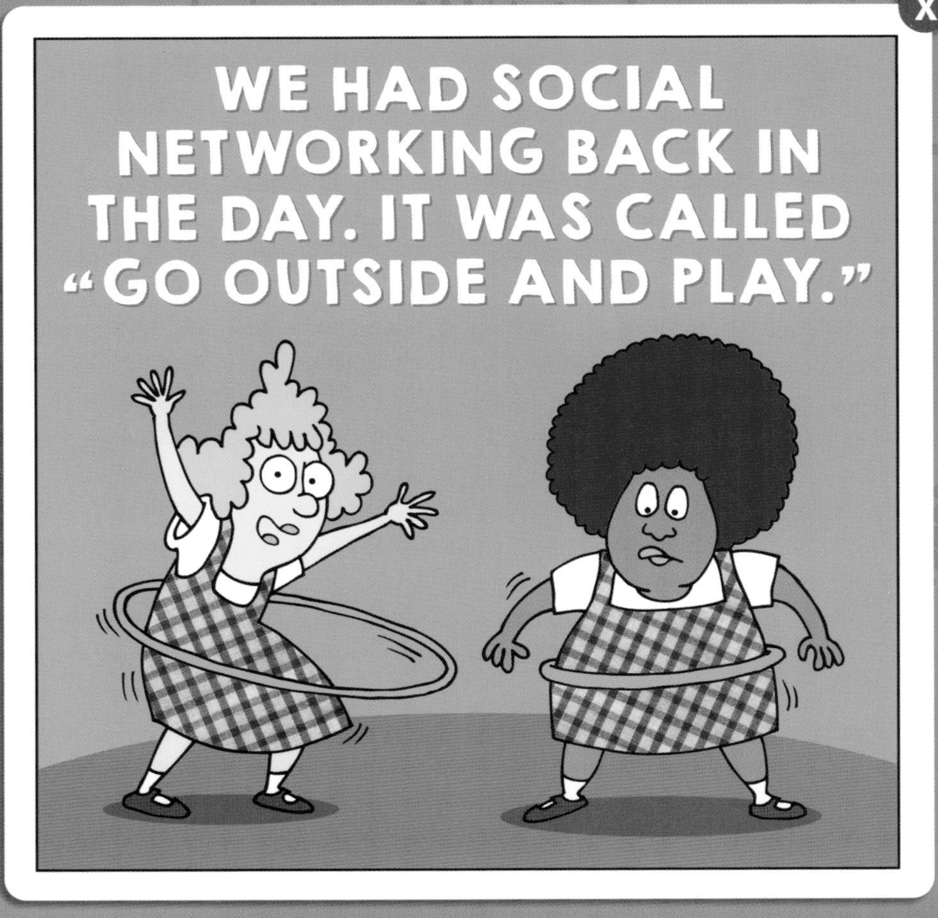
WE HAD SOCIAL NETWORKING BACK IN THE DAY. IT WAS CALLED "GO OUTSIDE AND PLAY."

LIFE IS SO BORING WHEN YOU DON'T HAVE AN ONLINE ORDER TO LOOK FORWARD TO.

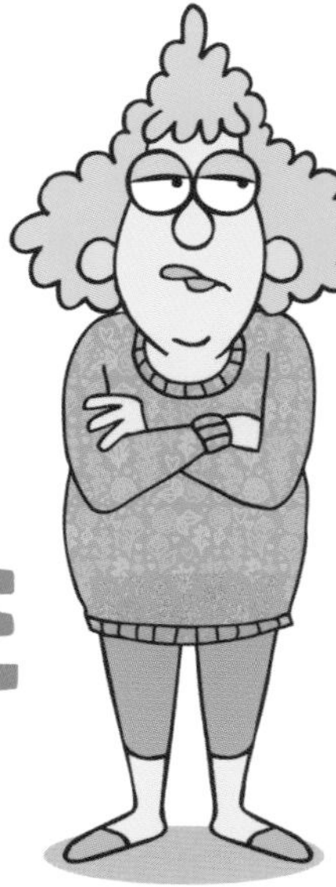

Exit Facebook, close laptop, get into bed, unlock phone, check facebook.

- True story.

X

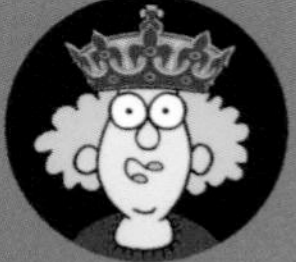

Hi again friends!

If you're reading this it means you've reached the end of the book and, if you made it through the whole thing without looking at your Facebook timeline, well done, you! You win a bunch of cookies—internet cookies that is—enjoy!

I hope my sassy sayings on all things social has entertained you and kept your scrollin' fingers busy while Walt was up on the roof fixin' the internet. Now how to get him down?

I could give him back his ladders, but what fun would that be? I'm gonna film it and stick it on YouTube—I have a feeling I'm gonna go viral!

Speak soon, BBFN (bye-bye for now).

Yours,

Aunty A x

First Edition
24 23 22 21 20   5 4 3 2 1

Published by
Gibbs Smith
P.O. Box 667
Layton, Utah 84041

1.800.835.4993 orders
www.gibbs-smith.com

Illustrations by
Dave Iddon @ Backland Media
Designed by Dave Iddon
Contributed material by Rachel Backland

Printed and bound in China

Gibbs Smith books are printed on either recycled, 100% post-consumer waste, FSC-certified papers or on paper produced from sustainable PEFC-certified forest/controlled wood source.
Learn more at www.pefc.org.

ISBN 13: 978-1-4236-5434-6